ISLE of WIGHT
Railways
Remembered

Plate 1 An Isle of Wight Central Railway train stands at Newport Station at the turn of the century hauled by 2-4-0T No. 8, which was built by Beyer Peacock and introduced in May 1898. This locomotive survived the Grouping to enter Southern Railway service before being withdrawn in November 1929

ISLE of WIGHT

Railways Remembered

Peter Paye

Oxford Publishing Co.

ISBN 0-86093-212-5

Typesetting by:
Aquarius Typesetting Services, New Milton, Hants.

Printed in Great Britain by:
Biddles Ltd., Guildford, Surrey.

Published by:
Oxford Publishing Co.
Link House
West Street
POOLE, Dorset

Plate 2 Pride of the Isle of Wight Railways, Beyer Peacock 2-4-0T *Sandown* stands on the goods shed road at Ventnor. Built at Gorton Works, Manchester and introduced into traffic in July 1864, she was withdrawn by the Southern Railway in May 1923. The copper-capped chimney and polished dome are reminiscent of the Island railway in their heyday and are evidence of the pride which was furnished by locomotive crews on their machines.

To Mum & Dad, (Ruby and George)
for their love of the Isle of Wight,
greatly enhanced by rail travel

Contents

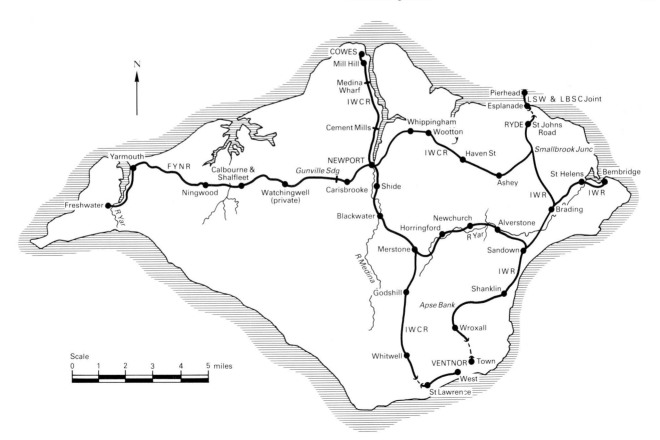

Plate 3 The epitome of an Isle of Wight train in the years before World War I. An Isle of Wight Central Railway Beyer Peacock 2-4-0T, No. 4 hauls a rake of five 4 wheel coaches between Newport and Ryde. The poor financial standing of the Island railways, and their reliance on buying second-hand vehicles from the mainland, is evident by the fact that the train is composed of an ex-LSWR brake third, two ex-LNWR composites, a North London Railway composite and an LSWR high roof third.

Introduction

The Isle of Wight, measuring some 23 miles, from the Needles in the west, to Bembridge Foreland in the east, and 13 miles north to south at its broadest, from Cowes to St. Catherine's Point has long been renowned as a holiday resort. Before Queen Victoria settled at Osborne, few could afford the visit across The Solent but the advent of the ferry, connecting the Island with the mainland gradually brought a change. By far the largest upheaval came with the building of railways on the Isle of Wight as the population increased, and holiday-makers swelled their ranks to sample the delights of downland scenery and sandy beaches. In 48 years, the 60 miles of coastline guarding 155 square miles of land became host to 55½ miles of railway serving 33 stations and 2 halts. However, the advent was far from smooth for the initial railways were mooted during the 'mania' of 1845. Opposition was vehement and one such scheme, to build a line from Ventnor to Cowes, with a branch from Newport to Ryde, brought avid protests from landed gentry including Sir Richard Simeon and Lord Yarborough, as well as from innkeepers, shop owners and some of the populus of Newport and Ryde. Undeterred promoters continued to strive and gradually opposition subsided until August 1859 when the first railway on the Island linking Cowes and Newport was authorized.

Thereafter, many railways were projected, but the final structure of the Island network was born from the ranks of eight separate companies.

Section	Railway Company	Date Opened
Cowes to Newport	Cowes & Newport Railway	16th June 1862
Ryde St. John's Road to Shanklin	Isle of Wight Railway	23rd August 1864
Shanklin to Ventnor	Isle of Wight Railway	10th September 1866
Sandown to Shide	Isle of Wight (Newport Junction) Railway	1st February 1875
Ryde St. John's Road to Newport	Ryde & Newport Railway	20th December 1875
Shide to Newport	Isle of Wight (Newport Junction) Railway	1st June 1879
Ryde St. John's Road to Ryde Pierhead	London & South Western Railway and London, Brighton & South Coast Railway Joint Committee	12th July 1880
Brading to Bembridge	Brading Harbour Improvement & Railway Company	27th May 1882
Newport to Freshwater	Freshwater, Yarmouth & Newport Railway	10th September 1888
Merstone to St. Lawrence	Newport, Godshill & St. Lawrence Railway	20th July 1897
St. Lawrence to Ventnor Town	Newport, Godshill & St. Lawrence Railway	1st June 1900

Ultimately the Cowes & Newport, Ryde & Newport and Isle of Wight (Newport Junction) railways amalgamated to form the Isle of Wight Central Railway in July 1887 and, in 1913, this company absorbed the Newport, Godshill & St Lawrence Railway. The Freshwater, Yarmouth & Newport Railway was worked by the IWCR until 1913 when, after a disagreement, the company operated its own services. The Isle of Wight Railway remained nominally independent and bought outright the Bembridge line in 1898, although it had worked the branch from the opening day.

By the turn of the century, the Isle of Wight was a popular holiday area, particularly the south-east coastal resorts of Sandown, Shanklin and Ventnor. In 1901, over 1,600,000 passengers and 200,000 tons of freight were carried on the railways and traffic continued to increase up to World War I. The Island railways, at this period, left much to be desired, however, for many locomotives and rolling stock were second hand from mainland companies, the permanent way was poor, services were infrequent with slow speeds and, in comparison with other systems, fares were expensive. Despite this, the railways had an individuality and charm of their own.

As a result of the Railways Act of 1922 the Southern Railway absorbed the IWR and IWCR on 1st January 1923 and, after some obstinacy, also absorbed the FYNR, from 1st August. The new regime replaced much of the ageing rolling stock and, with a steady modernization and rationalization programme, achieved, by the mid-1930s, standards of punctuality, cleanliness, speed and frequency of service which were unknown before.

Unfortunately, by this time, the improving internal combustion engine and all weather roads combined to increase the drift of traffic away from the railway. In October 1921, Dodson Brothers introduced a service of buses between Cowes and Newport under the name of Vectis Bus Company. Other routes were added and, on 27th August 1929, the Southern Vectis Omnibus Co. Ltd. was formed to acquire the business with the Southern Railway Company holding a 50 per cent interest.

After the improvements of the late 1920s and 1930s, little was added to the Island railway system and, despite great efforts, World War II took its toll and standards declined. From 1st January 1948, the railways were nationalized and, although holiday traffic picked up after the lean war years, patronage was rapidly dwindling. By 1951, the Island railway conveyed, annually an estimated 3,000,000 passengers compared with 17,600,000 carried by Southern Vectis and other bus companies. The figures were self explanatory, and reduction of the railway system appeared inevitable as most passengers were carried in the three months of high summer, leaving empty trains and little revenue for three-quarters of the year. Merstone to Ventnor West closed from 15th September 1952 and, amidst vehement protest, the Bembridge branch and the Newport to Freshwater line closed on 21st September 1953. Following a short reprieve, the Newport to Sandown line closed on 6th February 1956. Doctor Beeching finally sounded the death knell of the Smallbrook Junction to Newport and Cowes line on 21st February 1966. Later in the same year, on 18th April Shanklin to Ventnor services were withdrawn leaving steam traction to soldier on between Ryde Pierhead and Shanklin to the end of the year. The system was then closed for electrification work until it reopened, on 20th March 1967, using ex-London Transport rolling stock.

A portrayal of the final ten years of steam traction appeared in *Steam on the Isle of Wight (1956-66)*, published by Oxford Publishing Company. An attempt has been made in this, the companion volume, to show the character, quaintness and individuality of the Isle of Wight railways in bygone days, when the independent companies held sway, as well as showing the Southern era and the initial years of nationalization. If the illustrations in the book have evoked memories of an industrious yet relaxed era, when the railways were reshaping the destiny of the Island, then a visit to the Isle of Wight Steam Railway at Haven Street is recommended. On Thursdays and Sundays in high summer, the Wight Locomotive Society operates a service from Haven Street to Wootton, on the former Ryde to Cowes line. The Society is the owner of the sole surviving 02 class locomotive, No. 24 *Calbourne*, the ex-IWCR 'Terrier' No. 11 and ex-FYNR 'Terrier' No. 2, now numbered W8 *Freshwater*.

Plate 3

RYDE PIERHEAD

Plate 4 Ryde Pierhead Station was opened on 12th July 1880 by the London & South Western and London, Brighton & South Coast Railways' Joint Committee together with the line to St. John's Road. Ryde, the main gateway to the Isle of Wight for nearly two centuries, enjoyed a daily sailing boat service from Portsmouth as early as 1796. Due to the shallow nature of the foreshore, it was quickly realized that vessels could not offload at low tide. To obviate difficulties, in 1814 a promenade pier was opened and later a tramway structure. The increasing popularity of the Island as a holiday resort brought the extension of the railway to The Solent and the new railway pier was constructed alongside the existing pier.

The original Pierhead Station, shown in this September 1920 view, was built in a 'T' shape, with the buildings and concourse at the end of, and at right angles to, the three platforms. Platform 1 was on the western side with a timber-backed screen, whilst platforms 2 and 3 were each side of the island platform. These platforms were just over 400ft. in length and were of timber planking, with a timber canopy affording protection to passengers. The coaches standing at platform 1 are IWR Metropolitan bogie stock, whilst the trailing crossover which was situated between platforms 1 and 2 to enable locomotives to run round their trains, can be seen below the fourth vehicle.

Plate 5 An IWR train departs from platform 2 for Ventnor and passes Ryde Pierhead signal box. In this early 1900s view, can be seen the signal gantry which carried the starting signals for platform 2 and 3 only, platform 1 starting signal being located at the end of the platform.

Plate 6 In the early 20th century, considerable modification was carried out to the track layout and signalling at the Pierhead and, in this photograph dating from 1907, the permanent way staff who are renewing the crossover at the entrance to the station, have taken time off to pose for the photographer.

Plate 7 A view of the railway pier at Ryde showing the tall 'up' home signal gantry in advance of the signal box.

Plate 8 The 'up' home signal gantry was considerably reduced in height by the time the Southern Railway took over the Island's railway network. In this scene, photographed soon after the Grouping, an ex-IWR 2-4-0T is signalled for platform 3, with an 'up' train from Cowes. The leading vehicle is an ex-LSWR one compartment brake third (IWCR No. 12), and the remainder of the stock is an ex-LSWR 3 set (either No. 491 or 492) formed of a centre brake third, composite and an ex-Plymouth, Devonport and South Western Junction Railway brake third. In the foreground are the rails of the pier tramway, running alongside the railway pier on a separate structure. The system was initially worked by horse traction, introduced on 29th August 1864 for the benefit of passengers arriving by ferry from the mainland. In 1886, Siemens electric traction was introduced but this was replaced in 1927 by Drewry petrol railcars. These survived until closure of the tramway in January 1969.

Plate 9 At the Grouping, the need for more modern motive power on the Island was abundantly clear, for many locomotives had long passed their prime with the average age of 45½ years. Following an unsuccessful attempt by the IWCR to purchase an LSWR 02 class 0-4-4T, the Southern Railway transferred two Adams tanks to the Island in May 1923 to ease the motive power position. Nos. 206 and 211, still in London & South Western livery, were landed at Ryde Pierhead by the Admiralty floating crane from Portsmouth Dockyard. No. 211, fitted with Westinghouse pump attached to the left hand side of the smokebox, is raised aloft. To the lower right of the picture is No. 206.

Plate 10 Fifteen or so years later, 02 class 0-4-4T, No. 26 *Whitwell* working Ryde duty No.5, waits in platform 2 with a special departure for Ventnor. The burnished buffers and the polished brasswork on the locomotive is worthy of note. By this time, the Island had increased in popularity as a tourist resort and, in 1933 the Southern Railway rebuilt the station with four platforms. The leading coach on the train is thought to be a former GER vehicle, whilst the coach to the right is No. 4117, an ex-London, Chatham & Dover Railway eight compartment third.

Plate 11 The extensive alterations made to Ryde Pierhead Station were thought to have been originally mooted by the Chief Engineer of the L&SWR before the Grouping. The complete renewal of decking on both the railway and promenade piers preceded improvements to the station. Buildings were more extensive and station platforms were renewed by laying asphalt on concrete. Space was increased between the buffer stops and ticket barriers, to allow the movement of Lister trucks hauling baggage trolleys. The platforms were renumbered in reverse order, with No. 1 on the east side, with an engine water tank between 1 and 2 roads, and a water crane at end of platform 3. The new platforms were shorter than the original at 388ft. and were added to by platform 4 which was opened for traffic on 1st July 1933. This structure, 362ft. in length, was accommodated on the west side of the station by moving the original back screen outwards. The new station is seen in this view soon after opening with 02 class tank locomotives at the head of platforms 2 and 3. Platform 4 is to the left.

RYDE ESPLANADE

Plate 12 Ryde Esplanade, situated 32 chains from Ryde Pierhead, once established as a simple double line through station, became the busiest station on the Isle of Wight, catering for the thousands of passengers travelling to and from the mainland, as well as for the local populus journeying to other Island stations. The LSW/LBSC Joint Company never handled rail goods traffic and there were no sidings or goods yard. The signal box at the south end of the 'up' platform had a 12 lever frame, although 5 levers were spares. The box was not essential for the working of the line and was finally closed by the Southern Railway in 1923. In this view of Esplanade Station and Ryde Pier, an IWR train is leaving the 'up' platform past the ornate signal gantry which contained the Esplanade 'up' starting signal (the highest in the off position), and the three Pierhead distant signals, (the central also in the off position).

Plate 13 IWR 2-4-0T *Ryde,* resplendent with shining brass dome, approaches Ryde Esplanade with an extensive train of ten 4 wheel coaches. The leading vehicle is an ex-North London Railway five compartment low back third, whilst the rest of the train consists of IWR 1864 low roof stock. The signal in the foreground is the Ryde Pierhead 'up' fixed distant and is on the same post as the Esplanade starting signal (not shown in the photograph).

Plate 14 Still in LSWR livery after arrival on the Island in 1923, LSWR 02 Class 0-4-4T No. 211 (later No. W20 *Shanklin*) approaches Ryde Esplanade Station after running the 32 chains from Ryde Pierhead with a Ventnor train formed of an ex-IWR 1882 highroof 4 wheel, four compartment third followed by ex-IWR Metropolitan Railway coaches. To the left of the locomotive is the single lever ground frame, released by Annett's key, which was retained to operate the crossover at the North end of Esplanade Station during repairs or emergencies.

Plate 15 A glimpse over the fence at Ryde Esplanade Station sees IWCR 4-4-0T No. 6 waiting to depart with a Cowes train. The fireman had ensured a good head of steam as the safety valves had lifted. The advertisements on the fence date the photograph as 1924 with the Southern Railway offering cheap excursions on the Island.

Plate 16 In the pre-war years, E1 class 0-6-0T locomotives were often drafted in to assist on passenger work. No. 2 *Yarmouth* awaits departure from Ryde Esplanade with a Ventnor train.

RYDE ESPLANADE TO RYDE ST. JOHN'S

Plate 17 Making for Ryde Esplanade, an IWR 2-4-0T locomotive heads a rake of seven 4 wheel coaches around the 10 chain radius curve, near Monkton Mead Brook. The leading coach was originally a brake third, which was later converted by the IWR to a van, and is followed by three first/third composites, two four compartment seconds, all of 1864 vintage, and an 1882 vintage composite, either IWR No. 37 or 38. The body of No. 37 is now preserved at Haven Street Steam Centre.

RYDE ST. JOHN'S ROAD

Plate 18 An aerial view of Ryde in August 1933 with Ryde St. John's Road Station, works and locomotive depot shown in the left foreground. The curving nature of the railway route through the town, terminating at Ryde Pierhead at the top of the picture, can be easily traced.

Plate 19 Ryde St. John's Road Station, situated 1 mile 19 chains from Ryde Pierhead, was originally the terminus of the Isle of Wight (Eastern Section) Railway which opened on 23rd August 1864. The original platform, 212ft. in length, with the station building, was on the west side of the single line, but an additional platform was later located on the east side of a run-round loop. In 1869, the station building was extended and, two years later, the two platforms were lengthened. Little alteration was made when the Ryde to Newport Railway arrived on 20th December 1875. When the LSW & LBSC Joint line was opened to Ryde Pierhead in 1880, the platform on the eastern side was rebuilt in timber as an island platform for use by IWR trains and a footbridge was provided to give access to and from the platform on the western side. The Newport and Cowes train then used the western side platform only whilst the IWR had exclusive use of the eastern island platform, the single lines thence, to Smallbrook, being entirely independent. The Joint line committee installed their Ryde St. John's Road North signal box to control all points and signals on the Pierhead side of the station and this complemented Ryde St. John's Road South signal box which dated from the arrival of the R & NR line. This view shows St. John's Road Station, looking south, in 1900 with the IWR 'down' starting signals to the left and the IWCR 'down' starter on the right. Beyond the IWC starter is St. John's Road South signal box.

Plate 20 St. John's Road Station facing north, in 1900, with, from left to right, the IWC 'up' and 'down' single line, the IWR 'up' line and, on the other side of the island platform, the IWR 'down' line. Ryde Works, the windmill and hydraulic engine hoist are on the right, whilst in the background are the tall 'up' starting signals. The hump on the footbridge is the connection to St. John's Road overbridge, which was later removed.

Plate 21 Twenty years later, few alterations had been made. A 1920 view of the station, facing north from the island platform, also shows the building on the right which is the IWR Carriage & Wagon Shop.

Plate 22 The developing holiday business at resorts in the eastern side of the Isle of Wight was severely taxing the train services and, after the Grouping in 1923, the Southern Railway authorities sought a way of improving line capacity between Ryde and Ventnor. Part of the scheme involved the re-organization of running lines and signalling on the approach to Ryde, with an extension of full double line working during summer months from Ryde St. John's North box to Smallbrook, with the installation of a new signal box and scissors crossover at the latter point. The new signal box was opened on 18th July 1926, and two years later the running lines at Ryde St. John's were rearranged, station buildings and platforms were rebuilt and a new goods yard was provided. The original west side platform became the platform for 'up' trains, whilst the island platform handled 'down' services. A new signal box was erected near to the South box and the old South and North boxes were demolished. The new signal box was a standard SECR wooden structure which had been removed from Waterloo Junction and was provided with a 40 lever frame. The photograph shows work in progress on 8th November 1928 with the new concrete platforms in situ and both the new signal box and old South box extant.

Plate 23 The completed station, facing south in 1933, with No. W27 *Merstone* arriving with a train from Cowes. Smallbrook signal box is switched in for the signal gantry at the end of the 'down' platform which only displays the starter arms for the 'down' loop (left) and 'down' main lines (right). The train is formed of LCDR set No. 496, comprising brake thirds Nos. 4115 and 4116, seven compartment composite No. 6360 and third, No. 2433. The ex-LBSCR 10 ton wagons behind the fencing show the Lancing form of repaint after repairs with 'SR' on the middle three planks (first right) and Ashford repairs and repaint with 'SR' on the top three planks. The other open wagons are of IWR/IWCR origin.

RYDE ST. JOHN'S TO SMALLBROOK

Plate 25 Ryde St. John's goods yard. No. W25 *Godshill*, on Ryde duty No. 6, shunts a motley collection of passenger and freight vehicles, including ex-LSWR goods brake, or road van, No. 56053, with single verandah and ex-LCDR 4 wheel brake third, No. 4133 (formerly four compartment, rebuilt to two compartment in April 1934 for use on mail trains). These are followed by an LBSCR van for fish traffic, an ex-LCDR 4 wheel luggage van (either No. 1008/9 or 1013), an LBSCR 10 ton van for general traffic and an LBSCR 10 ton van for fish traffic. The seventh vehicle is an LSWR 4 wheel brake luggage van followed by seven LBSCR 10 ton open wagons.

Plate 26 An 02 class 0-4-4T, No. 19, departs from Ryde St. John's Road, in 1925, with a Ventnor train composed of an ex-IWR 1882 high roof 4 wheel composite, two four compartment thirds and four Metropolitan rigid bogie vehicles. In the background is an ex-LBSCR 10 ton open wagon, No. 26139, with curved endboards. An IWR grounded van body spans the stream on the right.

Plate 27 (above) Near the site of Smallbrook Junction, IWCR 'Terrier' No. 10 descends the 1 in 172 incline and makes for Ryde St. John's with a coal train from Medina Wharf, formed of mixed IWR and IWC open wagons.

BRADING

Plate 28 (left) An aerial view of Brading situated 4 miles 54 chains from Ryde Pierhead, photographed on 1st September 1928 and showing, in the left background, the junction station and small goods yard. In the foreground is the cement mill and its sidings on the Bembridge branch, with wagons being loaded with goods whilst, in the lower part of the picture, five 4 wheel coaches are stored.

Plate 29 (top right) An early view of the original building of the 'up' side platform at Brading, in the 1880s. Of particular interest is the oil lighting and the station clock which, according to Board of Trade Regulations, had to be visible to train crews and passengers.

Plate 30 (bottom right) Brading Station, around the turn of the century, with IWR 2-4-0T *Sandown* entering the 'down' platform with a Ventnor train formed of 1864 stock. A canopy has been added to the station building whilst a covered footbridge connects the platforms. The coaches of the Bembridge branch train are standing in the bay platform. Note the luxurious hedgerow, flowerbeds and gas lamps.

Station Isle of Wight

Plate 31 Brading Station, facing north, in 1913 with 2-4-0T *Bonchurch* seen entering the station with a Ventnor train, formed of an 1882 composite, two 1864 4 wheel four compartment seconds, a three compartment first, two three compartment composites, a guard's luggage van and a plain luggage van. *Bonchurch* sports a solid brass dome, whilst the safety valves are in the conventional position in front of the cab. Safety chains are also still fitted to the front buffer beam.

Plate 32 An O2 class 0-4-4T, No. 20, without name, and still equipped with a small bunker, is silhouetted against the skyline as she leaves Brading with a Ventnor to Ryde Pierhead train on 24th June 1928. The train is formed of ex-IWR Metropolitan Railway stock with an ex-LSWR 6 wheel arc roof guards van next to the engine. The home signal, on the left, is for trains on the Bembridge branch. The post also carries the Brading Quay distant (in the off position).

Plate 33 A busy time at Brading, in 1937, as 02 class No. 15 *Cowes* enters with a Ryde to Ventnor train whilst another 02 class locomotive waits for the road to Ryde St. John's. No. 19 *Osborne* shunts on to the Bembridge branch train. The lower quadrant signals remained in use until after World War II. To the left, the goods yard is host to a number of newly-painted vans.

Plate 34 The fireman of 02 class 0-4-4T No. 23 *Totland* surrenders the Ryde St John's to Brading single line token to the signalman as the train enters Brading with a Ryde Pierhead to Ventnor working, soon after World War II. The ex-IWR branch starting signal on the right is off, for the connecting Bembridge branch train to depart. The tall 'up' signal is of LSWR vintage and was provided by the Southern Railway when the line to Sandown was doubled. The leading vehicles are part of an LCDR 4 set, the third coach being a short all-steel clad composite. No. 23 *Totland* sports a wartime livery with 'sunshine' lettering.

Plate 35 From 1926, A1X class 0-6-0T locomotives were regularly drafted to work the Bembridge branch services, replacing the ageing ex-IWR 2-4-0Ts and ex-IWCR locomotive No. 5. An immaculate ex-IWCR 'Terrier' No. 11 *Newport* enters Brading, in the late 1920s, with the branch train consisting of LCDR 4 wheel vehicles. The middle coaches are a 2 set formed of a four compartment brake third and a composite. The leading coach is a five compartment third and the rear coach an LCDR brake luggage van.

Plate 36 The driver of A1X class 0-6-0T No. W13 *Carisbrooke* is evidently proud of his locomotive as she waits in the bay platform at Brading with a Bembridge branch train in the early 1930s. The locomotive is fitted with a copper-capped chimney and large bunker fitted to all Isle of Wight 'Terrier' tanks. When working the Bembridge services, these A1X class locomotives were allocated to Ryde Shed. The coaching stock is 4 wheel LCDR set No. 509 (2 set, three compartment brake third No. 4150 and composite No. 6393). The strengthening vehicles are also LCDR 4 wheelers.

SANDOWN

Plate 37 Sandown, 6 miles 41 chains from Ryde Pierhead, on the Isle of Wight main line, was the junction for the former Isle of Wight (Newport Junction) Railway, later IWCR branch to Newport, which curved away to the west along the valley of the Eastern Yar. When the IWR was opened, the head office was located adjacent to the station but this was soon moved to Ryde St. John's. An IWR 2-4-0T prepares to depart from the 'down' platform with a Ryde to Ventnor train, in 1910. The platform line on the left was used by IWCR trains.

Plate 38 Sandown Station, from the south, in 1920. The south end of both 'down' and island platforms have been extended some 30ft. in length necessitating the removal of the tree shown in the previous photograph. The signal box, perched high above the 'up' platform, afforded the signalman a good view of the station approaches. The main block of station buildings on the 'down' platform were connected to the 'up' side and bay platforms by a subway.

Plate 39 The exterior of Sandown Station in 1910. Inconveniently situated at the back of the town, and almost a mile from the sea front, necessitated conveyances for the arriving public. Two horse-drawn taxis of the period are shown waiting for patronage. The station was extensively modernized by the Southern Railway in 1939, although the buildings shown remain almost untouched to this day.

Plate 40 The former single line section of the IWR main line, from Brading to Sandown, was doubled and opened to traffic on 23rd June 1927 as part of the Southern Railway's improvement to accommodate additional traffic on the Ryde to Ventnor line. IWR 2-4-0T *Bonchurch* departs with an 'up' train on the 1 in 484/77 falling gradient on the single line section to Brading in 1912. The train is formed of an IWR luggage van, an IWR brake third, rebuilt as a guard's luggage van, and 1864 passenger carrying vehicles. The last vehicle is of ex-North London Railway vintage.

Plate 41   By the early 1930s, nearly all Ryde to Ventnor workings were in the capable hands of the 02 class 0-4-4T locomotives. No. W19 *Osborne* with MacLeod modified bunker, and in the charge of Driver 'Bogie' Willis, stands in the 'down' platform on Ryde duty 1, ready to climb the 1 in 80 incline to Lake Road Bridge with a train of bogie coaching stock (set No. 494). The leading vehicle is an ex-IWCR Midland Railway 12 wheel vehicle, (SR No. 6988), rebuilt on conventional 4 wheel bogies, whilst the rest of the set includes three LCDR bogie thirds and two IWCR short bogie coaches.

Plate 42   The IWCR approached Sandown from the west, climbing at 1 in 55/270/96 on a 16 chain right-hand curve, and utilized the back of the island platform. IWCR Beyer Peacock 2-4-0T No. 4 climbs the bank past the home signal, with a train from Newport, in 1910.

Plate 43 After running round its train, IWCR No. 4 eases on to her train in the bay platform at Sandown. This photograph was taken after the Grouping, on 11th June 1923.

Plate 44 Beyer Peacock No. 4 was obviously a popular choice on the Sandown to Newport line as she departs from Sandown with a four coach train in 1912. The two leading coaches are IWCR short bogies which were built by the Lancaster Carriage & Wagon Company in 1890 and are brake composite IWCR No. 35 and composite IWCR No. 34. The third vehicle is an ex-NLR 4 wheel third, and the last coach is an ex-LSWR 4 wheeler. The signal to the right, is the IWCR starter, whilst the IWR starter is to the left of the loco-motive. In the IWR goods yard on the left, an IWR car truck awaits loading.

Plate 45 IWCR Beyer Peacock 2-4-0T No. 7, in original condition, stands at Sandown Junction in 1910. The vintage station nameboard gives an impressive display of destinations to travellers on the rival IWR system.

Plate 46 This undated photograph shows an IWR 2-4-0T in a predicament, and receiving some attention at Sandown, after running through the buffer stops of the siding on the west side of the IWCR bay platform line. The locomotive, almost undamaged after landing in the soft earth, was later pulled back on to the track after temporary rails were laid.

Plate 47 An 02 class 0-4-4T, No. 24 shunts a rake of wagons and a brake van between the 'down' side (ex-IWR) yard to the ex-IWCR Newport line yard, at Sandown, on 1st November 1928.

SHANKLIN

Plate 48 Shanklin Station, situated 8 miles 28 chains from Ryde Pierhead, in a view facing Ryde, at the turn of the century. The station master and staff stand on the 'down' platform whilst two porters are handling luggage on the 'up' side. Originally, only the 'down' platform was provided when the line opened from Ryde St. John's in 1864. The 'up' platform was added in 1866, with the opening of the line to Ventnor.

Shanklin.

Plate 49   In November 1891, the Isle of Wight Railway commenced running an express service between Ryde Pierhead and Ventnor, to convey invalids from the mainland to the consumptive and other hospitals and homes in Ventnor. The train was requested by the local authority of Ventnor who also sought accelerated services between London and Portsmouth by the LSWR and LBSCR. The 12 miles 44 chains from Ryde Pierhead to Ventnor was scheduled for 21 minutes. The inaugural journey took only 19 minutes and in practice, timings of 17 to 18 minutes were quite common, as keen crews took advantage of not having to stop at intermediate stations. This was noteworthy running owing to the slacks required to interchange tokens at Brading, Sandown and Shanklin, followed by the 1½ miles of the 1 in 70 incline at Apse Bank. The train was lightly-loaded to four, 4 wheel coaches and a van; a tail load, weighing 42 tons. The train, hauled by 2-4-0T *Ryde*, with its distinctive headcode of a red disc with a white cross at the top of the smokebox door, crosses an 'up' train at Shanklin just prior to the withdrawal of the service in May 1898. After the withdrawal of the service, additional coaches were attached to normal service trains.

Plate 50 The rural scene around Shanklin, on 11th June 1910, is evident as IWR 2-4-0T *Bonchurch,* with its polished brass dome, starts the climb of Apse Bank with a freight train, consisting of four open trucks, a covered van and brake van. The line to the left served the Shanklin Gas Company sidings.

Plate 51 Immediately after arrival on the Island, the ex-LSWR 02 class locomotives were placed in service on the Ventnor line. No. 206 (later No. W19 *Osborne*), in immaculate South Western livery, pulls into the 'down' platform, with a Ryde Pierhead to Ventnor train on 14th June 1923. The ex-Metropolitan Railway non-bogie eight wheelers were originally purchased in 1914 by the IWR, and remained the stronghold on the Ventnor services until the late 1920s.

Plate 52 The ex-Metropolitan Railway vehicles were still in use on 18th July 1927 as 02 class 0-4-4T No. W23, (later *Totland*) stands at Shanklin with a six coach set, No. 485 and two additional 4 wheel vans at the tail end of the train. Compared with photographs taken at the turn of the century, the permanent way had been extensively relaid to enable the heavier locomotives to operate the service.

Plate 53 By the mid-1920s, the IWR 2-4-0T locomotives had been replaced by 02 class 0-4-4Ts on the Ventnor line. No. W24 rolls into Shanklin with a Ventnor to Ryde Pierhead train on 23rd June 1928. The two leading ex-LSWR 4 wheel vans on the train date from the 1890s, whilst the third vehicle is an ex-IWR Metropolitan 8 wheel vehicle.

APSE BANK

Plate 54 Almost half of the 1 in 70 climb of Apse Bank was in a cutting which reached a considerable depth in Sand Cutting, situated three quarters of a mile from Shanklin. An 02 class 0-4-4T, No. 25 *Godshill*, pounds up the gradient with a Ryde Pierhead to Ventnor train in the summer of 1934. The coaching vehicles are either set No. 491 or 492, formed of LSWR centre van brake third, LSWR composite, LCDR eight compartment third, LCDR seven compartment composite, LCDR eight compartment third, LSWR ex-PDSWJ brake third and an elliptical roof LSWR van.

WROXALL

Plate 55 The original IWR station at Wroxall, situated 11 miles 3 chains from Ryde Pierhead, is pictured shortly after opening in the 1870s, and before a canopy was built in front of the booking office. The adjacent hotel provided refreshments for intending or arriving passengers throughout the life of the station, whilst the notice board showing timetables, to the left of the booking office, is headed 'Isle of Wight & Newport Junction Railways'. The dark mass of Stenbury Down is seen in the background.

Plate 56 A 1920 view of the single platform on the 'up' side of the line at Wroxall, facing south. The hotel in the foreground has ivy growing up the wall whilst the booking office building has acquired a canopy affording passengers some shelter from the elements.

Plate 57 In 1925, the Southern Railway increased the line capacity of the Ryde to Ventnor route, for the improved summer service, by installing a crossing loop and a 'down' side platform at Wroxall. The crossing loop and new platform are shown in this photograph, taken in 1952 from almost the same angle as the previous picture. Note the ivy has now made a complete covering of the wall facing the 'up' platform.

WROXALL TO VENTNOR TUNNEL

Plate 58 From the end of Wroxall platform the Isle of Wight Railway line climbed at a gradient of 1 in 88 almost to the northern portal of Ventnor Tunnel. IWR 2-4-0T *Sandown* climbs the bank with a summer afternoon train from Ryde Pierhead. The ten 4 wheel vehicles on the train are, from the engine (1) 1864 composite, (2) 1864 third, (3) 1882 second, (4) 1882 composite, (5) 1882 second, (6) 1882 composite, (7) 1882 second, (8) 1864 composite, (9) brake luggage van, (10) unidentified van.

VENTNOR

Plate 59 When Ventnor Station first opened in 1866, only temporary accommodation was provided. The station was on the site of an existing quarry and, as can be seen from the photograph, quarrying was still much in evidence when the first trains ran. An IWR 2-4-0T, with original open cab, awaits departure with a train for Ryde formed of an original birdcage three compartment brake third and a first/third composite.

Plate 60 A later development to the facilities at Ventnor was the installation of a goods yard and coal ground for local merchants, who were accommodated in caves in the cliff to the left of the picture. The island platform is without cover although the main station platform has acquired a canopy. However, it is devoid of a back wall and must have been very draughty. A goods shed has also been provided at the back of the main platform but, in this picture, it is host to two 4 wheel coaches.

Plate 61 Ventnor Station, photographed from St. Boniface Down, in 1920. This view from the 'down' side of the line gives evidence of (by Island standards) the considerable coal traffic, dealt with by Jolliffe Brothers and Wood & Company at the station. The caverns and caves used as offices and stores can clearly be seen. By this period, the large goods shed was being used for its intended use.

Plate 62 Ventnor Tunnel (1,312 yards long) carried the line under St. Boniface Down and was constructed of a brick horseshoe arch with a 14ft. 2in. span diameter. The south portal, with the adjacent Ventnor signal box, in 1920, shows the semaphore signals located just beyond the tunnel mouth which, according to former Island enginemen, were difficult to locate especially if the tunnel was full of smoke. This picture makes an interesting comparison with the upper picture of page 74 of *Steam on the Isle of Wight (1956-66)* published by Oxford Publishing Company.

Plate 63 An unidentified IWR 2-4-0T enters Ventnor Station with a train from Ryde Pierhead in 1910.

Plate 64 Another comparison with the picture on page 40 of *Steam on the Isle of Wight (1955-66)* can be made with this view of a spotless No. W24, arriving at Ventnor with a train from Ryde in 1936. The burnished buffers and polished brass on *Calbourne* show the high standard of cleanliness maintained by footplate staff and cleaners before World War II.

Plate 65 IWR 2-4-0T *Wroxall* awaits departure with a Ryde train at the outer side of the island platform at Ventnor, circa 1906. The 4 wheel vans behind the locomotive are IWR No. 2 and then either Nos. 1, 3 or 4 built by Oldbury in 1864 and purchased new by the Company. These vans were originally brake thirds, but were rebuilt as vans in 1905 and survived to become part of the Southern fleet, but were withdrawn between 1925 and 1930. The remainder of the train is (3) 1864 first third composite, (4) 1864 three compartment first, (5 & 6) 1864 four compartment seconds, (7) 1864 composite, (8) three compartment first.

Plate 66 Beyer Peacock 2-4-0T *Ventnor*, stands at the water column at Ventnor in 1910. It was thought that limited bunker capacity of the IWR tank engines would require a top-up with coal at Ventnor, and the Company duly provided a coal stage. Evidently, the drivers thought differently as the coal stage shows little sign of use.

ST. HELEN'S

Plate 67 Soon after the IWR opened their line to Shanklin, a long siding was laid to serve the quay of the small harbour at Brading. Unfortunately, traffic was light as the sea access to the harbour was silting up and, as early as the seventeenth century, various speculators had sought schemes to drain and reclaim Brading marshes, by building a sea wall between St. Helen's and Bembridge. Efforts were unsuccessful until the Brading Harbour Improvement & Railway Company obtained powers, on 7th April 1874, to construct a 2½ mile railway from Brading to Bembridge across the reclaimed land. The scheme took eight years to complete and the new line, which initially followed the path of the original siding and formed a trailing connection to the 'down' main line, which precluded through running to Ryde, was opened on 27th May 1882 being worked under contract by the IWR. Leaving Brading, the Bembridge branch negotiated a 16 chain radius right-hand curve, past Brading Cement Company's siding, before following a mainly straight and level course to St. Helen's, 1 mile 51 chains from Brading, where the 232ft. platform, on the 'down' side of the line, was host to substantial red brick station buildings. The signal box at St. Helen's controlled the signals and points to St. Helen's Quay. This view shows St. Helen's Station in 1920, facing Brading. The water column was for the use of locomotives which were shunting the Quay.

Plate 68   In 1936, the turntable at Bembridge was enlarged to accommodate the 02 class 0-4-4T locomotives. During the conversion work, the branch was worked by a push-pull set, formed of two ex-LCDR 4 wheel vehicles, seen here leaving St. Helen's for Bembridge on 11th April, pushed by AIX class 0-6-0T No. 13 *Carisbrooke*. Set No. 484, comprised brake third No. 4112, originally built as a 6 wheeler No. 219 in 1898, and composite first class compartment and third saloon No. 6369, originally built as a 6 wheeler first class No. 20 in 1887. This set, together with set No. 483, were landed at St. Helen's Quay on 31st August 1924 and were primarily for use on the Ventnor West branch. Both sets, Nos. 483 and 484, were withdrawn in 1938.

Plate 69   Ex-IWCR 'Terrier' tank No. W9, still running as an A1 class, pulls into St. Helen's Quay with a freight soon after the Grouping in 1925. No. 9 suffered damage at Ryde Shed on 26th March 1926 and was condemned the following month. In the background is the gas house.

ST. HELEN'S QUAY

Plate 70 A view of the sidings at St. Helen's Quay from the level crossing in 1920. The weighbridge is to the left. Installations in the yard included a large goods shed and an engine shed, which was surmounted by a water tank. In independent days, the engine shed originally housed the Manning Wardle saddle tank *Bembridge*. The quayside boasted two cranes, one which was hand-operated and one mobile steam crane which ran on its own crane road, 320ft. long. At one time, a narrow gauge track, of 1ft. 11½in. gauge, crossed at right angles from the quayside to the gasworks and conveyed coal and coke in small tipper wagons.

Plate 71 A view of St. Helen's Quay, facing the station (in left background). To the left, the 300ft. long engineer's siding is occupied by match wagons, two open wagons and a steam crane. The No. 8 road is 440ft. long and the straight road, 600ft. in length. To the right is the crane road situated alongside the quay.

Plate 72 The north side of the quay, with a barge alongside the tranship goods shed. The quay was normally used for offloading coal, roadstone and machinery but, after the rebuilding of Medina Wharf in 1928, trade gradually declined in favour of the more modern equipment, until after World War II when St. Helen's became synonymous as a dumping ground for derelict coaching and wagon stock.

BEMBRIDGE

Plate 73 A Manning Wardle 0-6-0 tank *Bembridge*, with top hinge smokebox door, stands at Bembridge on the branch train in 1911, by which time the copper-capped chimney, which had been originally fitted, had been replaced by an ugly stove pipe design. The leading coach is an IWR five compartment low back third, followed by the ex-Ryde Pier tram, converted for use on the Bembridge line. The signal box is adjacent to the station building.

Leaving St. Helen's, the branch continued around a sharp right-hand 10 chain radius curve to run, for some distance, parallel to the toll road to Bembridge where, in later years, an array of houseboats could be seen flanking the harbour. As the line swung left, on a 20 chain radius curve, it climbed slightly to cross the Eastern Yar by a steel bridge and bisected an area known as Bembridge Lagoon. Nearing the terminus, the branch followed a sinuous course round a 17 chain left-hand curve, followed by a 16 chain right-hand bend, to enter Bembridge Station, 2 miles 61 chains from Brading, on a 1 in 600 rising gradient. The layout at Bembridge consisted of a 220 ft. long platform on the 'down' side of the single line which was host to the extensive and ornate station buildings. Also on the 'down' side of the line, west of the platform, was the 120ft. long orchard siding which served a coal wharf. Locomotives ran round their trains by using the turntable which, from 1936, was 25ft. in diameter, and the 231ft. long run-round loop on the 'up' side of the platform road. The layout was completed by a single yard siding, 200ft. long, which also served coal merchants and was used for general freight items.

Plate 74 A picturesque scene at Bembridge, around the turn of the century, with IWR 2-4-0T *Shanklin* arriving with a mixed train formed of three Brading Harbour Railway vehicles, allegedly ex-Ryde Pier, a 4 wheel open end luggage van, a pair of 6 wheel saloon coaches, with open end balconies guarded by iron railings, and a standard IWR five compartment third. The open wagons in the sidings are all IWR and include a 4 plank open, with dumb buffers, two 5 plank wagons with spring buffers, a 4 plank and a 7 plank with end door.

Plate 75 No. W13 *Ryde*, with the ex-IWCR railmotor coach, stands at Bembridge on 24th May 1930. Behind the coach can be seen the roof of the signal box.

Plate 76 Beyer Peacock tank *Wroxall* stands on the yard road at Bembridge in 1926. *Wroxall* was the last locomotive to carry the IWR red livery and looks out of place amidst goods and passenger vehicles which are painted in the new Southern Railway livery. The novel rail stop block, near the locomotive's driving wheels is worthy of note. Placed across the track, it effectively stopped the runaway movement of any vehicle in the siding. The branch route headcode carried by *Wroxall* was introduced by the Southern Railway in 1923.

Plate 77 The Bembridge branch was often worked by locomotives with high mileage requiring shops attention or by those nearing withdrawal. Beyer Peacock No. 8 was no exception and worked out its last days on the Bembridge branch. No. 8 is shown leaving the terminus for Brading with the branch train in the summer of 1929. By November of the same year, it was withdrawn for scrapping. The coach behind the locomotive is an ex-Great Eastern Railway five compartment 4 wheel third, followed by the ex-IWCR railmotor, SR No. 4103.

Plate 78 Ex-IWR 2-4-0T No. 13 *Ryde* awaits departure from Bembridge on 7th July 1928. The leading vehicle of the train is the ex-IWCR railmotor coach, whilst the open wagon in the siding is of LBSC origin and is shown prior to the end being cut down square with the sides. Driver Vallender, in charge of No. 13, is passing the time of day with a member of the station staff.

Plate 79 Once the Southern Railway absorbed the Island system, the 'Terrier' tanks were soon drafted to the more lightly laid lines, including Ventnor West, Freshwater and Bembridge. Because of a general locomotive shortage, the ex-IWCR members of the class were later joined by three which were transferred from the mainland; Nos. W3 in May 1927, W4 *Bembridge* in May 1929 and a new W9 *Fishbourne* in May 1930. No. W3, which was later named *Carisbrooke,* is shown at Bembridge on 6th June 1931 working her duty on the branch. In April 1932 she was renumbered W13 to make way for one of the E1 class 0-6-0 tanks which was transferred to the Island.

Plate 80 By May 1936, with the arrival of four additional 02 class locomotives, bringing the total to twenty on the Island, it was possible to return four 'Terrier' tanks back to the mainland, leaving only 3 AIX class locomotives on the Island. In the same month, on the Bembridge branch, the track had been strengthened and the turntable enlarged so the branch duty was covered by an 02 class 0-4-4T No. 19 *Osborne* which tested the turntable on 17th May 1936 and, afterwards, and for much of 1937, No. 23 *Totland* was the branch regular. No. 24 waits to depart the terminus in 1936.

ASHEY

Plate 81 When the Ryde & Newport Railway opened to traffic on Monday, 20th December 1875, the line was single track throughout with the only crossing loop located at Ashey, 2 miles 52 chains from Ryde St. John's Road. From the 'down' loop, a siding ran south through a chalk quarry under Ashey Down and this also served an adjacent racecourse. This view, facing Newport, showing the original layout, was photographed in the early 1920s.

Plate 82 The improvements made by the Southern Railway, and the increased Ryde to Ventnor and Ryde to Newport services, necessitated the installation of a signal box at Smallbrook, 1 mile 61 chains east of Ashey. The new signal box opened during summer months only and rendered the loop at Ashey inconvenient for operating purposes. After a new loop line was opened at Haven Street, in July 1926, the 'down' loop line at Ashey was converted to a siding and the signals, points and 12 lever frame were abolished. This view, facing Newport, shows the station in the 1950s almost unchanged except for the raised platform extension installed by the Southern Railway.

Plate 83 The impressive double storey red brick station building, which was provided on the 'up' platform as Ashey, together with the booking office and transit shed, appeared out of place in such a rural setting. It is thought the grandiose buildings were provided for the benefit of Sir Henry Oglander, of nearby Nunwell, who sold much of his land to the railway, and also for visitors to the local racecourse which was located south of the railway and which closed in 1929. This view of the station was taken just before the removal of the loop line.

Plate 84 A busy time at Ashey on 16th July 1925 as ex-IWCR 2-4-0T No. 7 enters the 'up' loop with a Newport to Ryde train, past an unidentified and, as yet, unnamed 02 class 0-4-4T, waiting to depart for Newport.

HAVEN STREET

Plates 85, 86 & 87 From Ashey, the line descended at a gradient of 1 in 87 before levelling out and then falling at 1 in 210 across open farmland. A descent at 1 in 70 for half a mile brought the line to Haven Street. The original station at Haven Street was a simple structure on the north side of the line, 3 miles 25 chains from Smallbrook. In 1886, a small gasworks was opened opposite the station and a siding was installed for the regular receipts of wagons of coal. Although the gasworks closed in the 1920s, the siding remained until 1966. In July 1926, a new crossing loop was opened by the Southern

Railway. This involved the removal of the old station buildings, shown in the upper photograph taken in 1910, and the installation of a new loop line behind the platform. Set back from the line, on the north side, was the garden landscape. A new single storey red brick building was erected which housed the waiting-room and signal box. A view facing Ashey of the island platform and the new station building (centre) and, facing Wootton (below) with the siding on the left. This station is the headquarters of the Isle of Wight Steam Railway and services are operated on Thursdays, and Sundays, during the summer months, to Wootton.

WOOTTON

Plate 88 Leaving Haven Street, the railway climbed initially at an incline of 1 in 68, followed by a short level section. Negotiating woodland and then farmland, the climb continued at 1 in 210/360/180/100/70 to Wootton. The station at Wootton was situated 7 miles 2 chains from Ryde Pierhead on the 'up' or north side of the line, with staff accommodation and the booking office beneath the arch of the adjacent road bridge. The station master's house was built in 1907, alongside, and level with, the road and five years later, the platform was extended, at the west end, to accommodate longer trains. This view, facing Newport, was photographed in the 1920s. Wootton Station was finally closed to traffic on 21st September 1953 after the earth movements.

Plate 89 Wootton Station, facing Haven Street, showing the booking office and waiting-room beneath the arch of the bridge.

Plate 90 A view of Wootton Station, facing Whippingham, showing the extension provided by the Southern Railway and the ornate oil lamps which provided illumination on the platform. The embankment opposite the platform was formed of a particularly slippery clay, which often caused problems to permanent way staff.

WHIPPINGHAM

Plate 91 Whippingham Station, situated 7 miles 63 chains from Ryde Pierhead, was opened by the Ryde & Newport Railway in 1875, although the passing loop was not added until 1912. Although remotely situated, the station was built on a grandiose scale as it served nearby Osborne House, the Island residence of Queen Victoria, some 2½ miles to the north. Although a public station, many visitors to the Royal Estate alighted here. This view, facing Wootton, shows the original platform which became the 'up' platform with the opening of the loop, and the 'down' platform to the right.

Plate 92 A view of Whippingham in early Southern Railway days, facing east, showing the flat-bottomed track still in use. The 'up' platform, host to the main station buildings and station master's house, was 234ft. long, whilst the 'down' platform, containing a small waiting hut was 242ft. in length. The platform was considerably shortened by British Railways soon after nationalization and the station closed on 21st September 1953, although the crossing loop remained in use until 1956.

Plate 93 The imposing red brick station buildings and station house on the 'up' platform at Whippingham. The booking office and waiting-room are adjacent to the station house. Unfortunately, due to its isolated position, nearly three miles from Whippingham village, during the post-World War II years, the number of passengers using the station was reduced to a mere handful each week.

Plate 94 Having descended the 1 in 64 incline from Wootton, 02 class No. 34 *Newport* enters Whippingham with a Ryde Pierhead to Cowes train on 27th June 1953. No. 34 was the first 02 class locomotive to be condemned, along with No. 23, in August 1955.

Plate 95 No passengers await No. 25 *Godshill* with her three coach Cowes to Ryde Pierhead train, as it pulls into Whippingham, in June 1953. The shortened 'down' platform, much rebuilt by British Railways, is on the left.

NEWPORT

Plate 96 From Whippingham Station, the line descended at a gradient of 1 in 460/L/340/147/L/87/65 to Newport Station, 9 miles 77 chains from Ryde Pierhead, the administrative headquarters of the Isle of Wight Central Railway and later the Southern Railway offices for the Island. The offices were situated on the first floor of the main station building, shown, in this view, from the approach road, in September 1920.

Plate 97 The original Cowes & Newport Railway station was a simple wooden single platform structure on the site of the goods yard but, on amalgamation with the Ryde & Newport, and later the absorption of the Isle of Wight (Newport Junction) Railway, an imposing new station was provided with two through platforms, an 'up' side loop platform and, at the north end of the 'down' platform a bay which was later utilized by Freshwater branch services. The station, viewed from the north in IWCR days, shows the elevated position of the railway above the town.

Plate 98 The C & N and R & N Joint Committee was authorized, by Act of Parliament in 1877, to construct a coal wharf on the River Medina near Cowes and, soon after completion, freight traffic began to increase. Because of the restricted space available at the new Medina Wharf, wagon loads were brought to Newport for marshalling and forwarding to various destinations on the Island. Additional land was purchased by the Joint Committee, and later the IWCR, to accommodate these sidings and this view, facing north from Newport in the 1930s, shows, from left to right, the carriage sidings and connecting line to the FYNR which were controlled by Newport North signal box. The 'down' and 'up' lines, to and from Cowes, are in the centre whilst, to the right, are Nos. 1 to 5 goods sidings and on the far right are the IWCR carriage sheds.

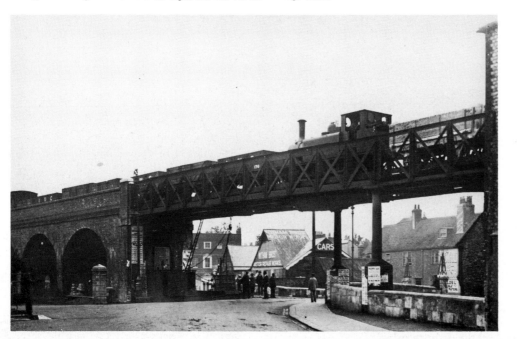

Plate 99 An IWCR 'Terrier' 0-6-0T shunts chalk wagons between Shide and Cement Mills siding over the Sandown line overbridge south of Newport in September 1920. This working was almost exclusively handled by 'Terrier' tanks because of the lightly laid track at each terminal which precluded the use of heavier locomotives.

Plate 100 Immediately south of Newport Station, the railway crossed the navigable River Medina by way of a viaduct which was built in 1875 by Campbell Johnson Ltd. for the R & NR (left) and (right) by Vospers of Gosport for the IW(NJ)R. A hand-operated drawbridge allowed shipping to pass upstream with the two separate sections of track sliding on rollers. The operation required the unbolting of fishplates and the disconnection of signal wires before movement could be made. During the early years of the railway, the span was opened several times daily, but use gradually dwindled after World War I although, in the late 1920s, sailing barges still required to negotiate the span. As can be seen, the movement of the span required the presence of several permanent way staff and was a costly operation. Newport South signal box is on the right.

Plate 101 An AIX class locomotive, No. 8 *Freshwater* passes Newport 'A' (formerly South) box, and approaches Newport Station with a train of chalk from Shide pits to Cement Mills. All the open wagons are privately-owned, the first, fourth and seventh being painted for the Vectis Cement Company, whilst the remainder are in the later Portland Cement Company's livery. The wagons were originally fitted with a handbrake on one side only and the end doors were at the Cowes end of the train to facilitate offloading at Cement Mills.

Plate 102 Isle of Wight Central Railway motive power awaits departure from Newport in 1906. On the right is A1 class 'Terrier' 0-6-0T No. 9 receiving a welcome topping up of water, whilst Black Hawthorn 4-4-0T, No. 6 awaits the 'right away' with a Cowes to Sandown train.

Plate 103 A similar view, of 02 class locomotives, many years later, in the 1930s. No. W30 *Shorwell* waits in the back platform with a Cowes to Ryde train whilst No. W27 *Merstone* also fitted with a Drummond type boiler, with safety valves in the dome, prepares to depart for Sandown. No. W27, in immaculate condition, is still fitted with a small bunker and coal rails. The footbridge connecting the platform is completely enclosed.

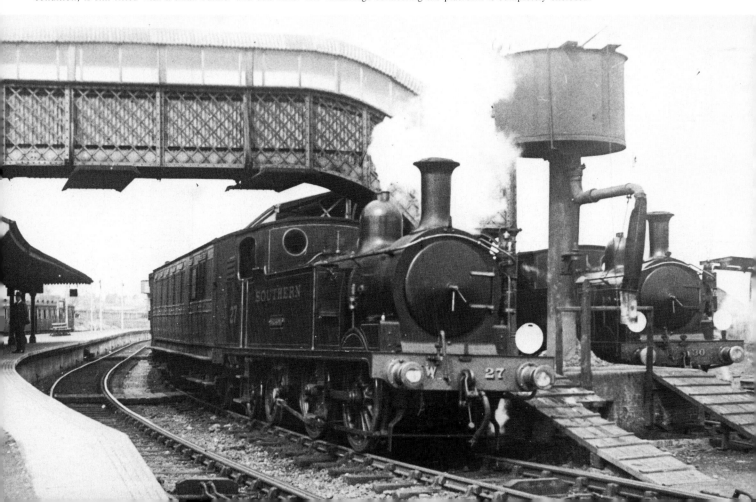

Plate 104 Newport Station, facing south, in 1910. The flat-bottomed track is ballasted to rail top level. IWCR 'Terrier' 0-6-0T No. 11 waits at the platform with a Sandown to Cowes train formed of an ex-LSWR two compartment brake third, followed by vehicles of former LNWR, LSWR and GER ownership. The main station building housed the general offices of the IWCR whilst below at platform level, the bookstall has an extensive array of literature for the discerning traveller.

Plate 105 LBSCR 4 wheel stock is still in evidence eighteen years later, on 6th November 1928, as ex-FYNR 'Terrier' No. 2 *Freshwater*, with nameplate located above the running number, takes water at the platform before setting off for Freshwater. In the rear platform, stands 02 class 0-4-4T No. 31, as yet unnamed.

Plate 106 An E1 class 0-6-0T No. ? *Yarmouth* swings round the curve pas Newport 'A' signal box and enter Newport Station with a train of vans from the Sandown line.

Plate 107 After absorption of the FYNR by the Southern Railway from 1st August 1923, ex-IWCR 'Terrier' No. 10 was allocated to Freshwater branch services rendering the Manning Wardle locomotive No. 1, surplus. By May 1924, No. 1 lost its steam brake and vacuum ejectors and was sent to work on shunting duties at Medina Wharf and trip workings to Newport. No. 1, in Southern livery and named *Medina*, pulls past Newport North signal box with a coal trip in 1931.

Plate 108 In the early 1930s, 02 class 0-4-4T No. W29 *Alverstone*, with its small bunker, approaches Newport with a Cowes to Ryde Pierhead train. No. W29 has a Drummond pattern boiler with dome top lock-up safety valve. The fish van to the right is No. 46958.

Plate 109 The 'Terrier' 0-6-0T locomotives were regularly used on the Freshwater branch workings but, as trains increased in weight, the diminutive locomotives were severely taxed on the undulatory gradients and were prone to priming. In 1931, it was decided to allocate the two remaining ex-IWR 2-4-0T locomotives, Nos. W13 and W16 to Newport, to work the line. Although near the end of their life, they proved to be competent for their task until withdrawn from service in 1933. No. W16 *Wroxall*, with the appropriate Freshwater line headcode, having reversed out of the bay platform at Newport, sets off for Freshwater with ex-LBSCR Stroudley 4 wheel close-coupled four coach set No. 495, formed of brake third, composite, third, and brake third, in 1932.

Plate 110 Newport North, in 1935, and 'Terrier' No. 8 *Freshwater* has arrived with a train from Freshwater and is waiting to propel the vehicles back into the 'up' bay platform at Newport. The train is formed of all LCDR coaches, a 4 set, with additional five compartment thirds. The signal to the left is an LSWR lattice post, installed by the Southern Railway, whilst the others have IWCR wooden posts. The line to the right, behind the signal box, is a siding.

CEMENT MILLS

Plate 111 An 02 class 0-4-4T, No. W29 *Alverstone*, trundles along with a Cowes to Ryde Pierhead train of 4 wheel vehicles, near Newport, on 20th May 1933. The leading vehicle is an ex-LSWR 4 wheel full brake, followed by an LCDR 4 wheel van, an LCDR 4 set of 4 wheelers and, lastly, a five compartment 4 wheel LCDR coach.

MEDINA WHARF

Plate 112 Situated on the 'up' side of the single line between Newport and Cowes, on the west bank of the river, was Medina Wharf. Originally opened in 1878 by the R & N and C & N Railways Joint Committee for unloading of coal and merchandise, it was extensively rebuilt by the Southern Railway in 1928 when the track layout was rearranged. This aerial view, looking towards Newport, shows the approach lines and sidings with the main line from Newport to Cowes in the right background.

Plate 113 After the Southern Railway transferred four ex-LBSCR E1 class 0-6-0T locomotives to the Island in 1932/3, the class quickly settled down to handle most of the heavy freight diagrams. No. W2 *Yarmouth* is seen passing Newport North 'up' distant, alongside the River Medina, with a coal train from Medina Wharf to Newport on 20th May 1933.

Plate 114 The old timber wharf which was replaced by a concrete structure in 1928. Coal, which had been brought direct from the coalfields of the north-east, is being craned out of the hold of the *Camberway* into wagons, in 1926. The flat-bottomed track necessitated the use of light axle weight locomotives for shunting Medina Wharf.

Plate 115 The junction to Medina Wharf from the main single line, 12 miles 68 chains from Ryde Pierhead, was controlled by a ground frame. E1 class 0-6-0T No. W4 *Wroxall* approaches the junction with a heavy coal train bound for Newport shortly after the locomotive was transferred to the Island in 1933. The main Newport to Cowes line is in the foreground.

Plate 116 Prior to the Grouping, locomotives and rolling stock, which were transferred to the Island railways, were conveyed either to St. Helen's Wharf on the IWR or to Medina Wharf. In 1923 however, some items of rolling stock were offloaded at Ryde Pierhead. By 1925, the Southern Railway had acquired a 150 ton floating crane and this was used subsequently for transferring locomotives and rolling stock to the Island via Medina Wharf. Ex-LCDR 6 wheel, converted to 4 wheel, brake third No. 4121 is lowered on to the wharf in 1926, whilst composite No. 6374, and another vehicle, await unloading.

Plate 117 In March 1926, an Adams 02 class 0-4-4T, already painted, fitted with Westinghouse brake equipment, and renumbered W28 at Eastleigh, awaits unloading from the floating crane with brake No. 1254.

MILL HILL

Plate 118 Mill Hill Station, situated 13 miles 68 chains from Ryde Pierhead, was located on a sharp 10 chain radius left-hand curve at the southern end of Mill Hill Tunnel (208 yards long). Opened in 1880 by the IWCR, it served the residential area at the back of Cowes. Originally a short siding was located on the 'up' side of the line.

COWES

Plate 119 The C & N Railway, later IWCR, terminus at Cowes, 14 miles 24 chains from Ryde Pierhead, was situated on an 8 chain radius curve on a falling gradient of 1 in 67/108 towards the buffer stops. 'Terrier' No. 10, standing in the platform, waits to depart with a Sandown train in 1906. The fireman has built a good fire as the safety valves are lifting. The distinctive light and dark painting of the valencing over the platform is of particular interest. The four coach train is formed of (1) LSWR four compartment 4 wheel low arc roof third (2) 4 wheel LSWR five compartment third (3) four compartment LSWR 4 wheel composite (4) LSWR 2 compartment brake third.

Plate 120 A Sandown train formed of ex-LSWR flat roof coaches, arrives at Cowes, platform 2, hauled by Beyer Peacock 2-4-0T No. 7. IWCR 10 ton open wagon No. 198 stands in the 320ft. dock siding on the right. This wagon was one of a batch built by Harrison & Cawson Ltd. and was purchased in 1897. The track layout was altered in 1918 when the end-on siding to the platform was removed. Cowes signal box was equipped with a 22 lever frame.

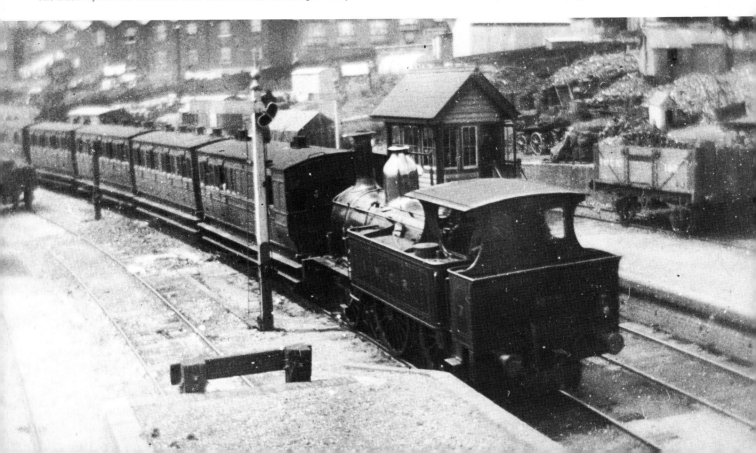

Plate 121 The altered layout at Cowes is evident in this 1931 photograph of a train from Ryde Pierhead arriving at platform 1, hauled by an 02 class tank with small bunker. Cowes Station was unfortunately inconveniently situated away from the waterfront, a good distance from the ferry terminal to the mainland and, consequently, in later years, passenger traffic suffered.

Plate 122 On a sunny 30th October 1928, 02 class 0-4-4T No. W30, later named *Shorwell*, waits to depart for Ryde Pierhead with a short three coach train. The footbridge crossing the station did not connect the platforms but maintained a public right of way between Cross Street and Terminus Road which was severed when the station was built. The method used for the locomotive to run round the train at Cowes was of interest and is fully described on pages 60 and 61 in *Steam on the Isle of Wight (1956-66)* published by Oxford Publishing Company. The train is an LSWR 3 set with a centre van brake third with an equalizing bogie next to the engine.

SANDOWN TO ALVERSTONE

Plate 123 IWCR 2-4-0T No. 4, complete with copper-capped chimney, approaches Sandown with a rake of five 4 wheel coaches in the 1920s. The leading coach is a GER five compartment third, followed by an NLR five compartment composite, two LNWR composites and an LSWR two compartment brake third.

ALVERSTONE

Plate 124 A 2-4-0T, No. 4, approaches the IWCR rebuilt platform at Alverstone, situated 1 mile 34 chains from Sandown, with a Sandown to Newport train. Although the corrugated waiting shelter and wooden fencing remain, the original wooden platform has been replaced by earth and clinker, with timber fencing. The original small station house has also been replaced by a more modern structure.

Alverstone Railway Station near Sandown

Plate 125   Alverstone Station, facing Newport, in 1920. 'Terrier' 0-6-0T No. 11 pulls into the crowded platform with a Newport to Sandown train, the leading coach of which is an ex-LBSCR brake. To the right can be seen the short goods siding, crossing the wooden bridge, over the adjacent stream which ran parallel to the track.

Plate 126   Alverstone station, facing Newport, in 1920. The 185ft. long station platform represented a neat appearance, with whitened edging, although the grand impression presented by the brick station house and booking office is rather let down by the corrugated iron structure on the platform, the nearer one being a waiting shelter and the structure beyond, a gentlemen's toilet.

NEWCHURCH

Plate 127 The original station house provided at Newchurch was similar to that at Alverstone, the platform being on the south side of the line with the building standing adjacent to the level crossing at the west end of the 228ft. long platform. Newchurch, however, boasted a large wooden waiting shelter and shed instead of the corrugated iron structure. As with other stations on the line, the platform was constructed of timber on brick and timber piling. This photograph, taken around the turn of the century, shows the very light flat-bottomed permanent way.

Plate 128 A 'down' train, hauled by 02 class 0-4-4T No. W25 *Godshill* arrives at Newchurch in 1932. Newchurch Station, 2 miles 45 chains from Sandown, was half a mile north of the village which was on a hill above the Eastern Yar Valley.

Plate 129 Newchurch Station, facing Newport. The 220ft. long single siding, serving the goods yard, handled vegetables, flowers and later sugar beet traffic from growers in the Arreton Valley but, after the 1930s, this declined in favour of the relatively few wagons of domestic coal or horticultural coke. Newchurch had the distinction of being an intermediate block post for train staff and ticket working between Sandown and Merstone, but the small signal box was later replaced by a ground frame.

Plate 130 Newchurch Station, facing Sandown, showing the siding and the open flat land through which the line ran. In the background is the outline of Brading Down.

Plate 131 The level crossing gates, station buildings and entrance to the goods yard at Newchurch in a view facing Newport.

HORRINGFORD

Plate 132 Away from Newchurch, the railway continued on level track before climbing for half a mile at 1 in 600/300 alongside the River Yar to Horringford, 3 miles 53 chains from Sandown, and situated alongside the main Sandown to Newport road a mile south of Arreton village. The platform, 180ft. in length, was west of the crossing on the south or 'down' side of the line. The goods yard, served by a single siding 317ft. in length, west of the station, handled similar commodities to Newchurch. This view faces Sandown, and an 02 class locomotive pulls into the station with a Sandown to Newport train in 1955.

Plate 133 A view facing east from Horringford showing the level crossing gates which protected the main Sandown to Newport road. Beyond the crossing is the home signal and, to the right, is the small signal box.

Plate 134 A view looking towards Merstone, showing the goods yard and 317ft. long Siding which, in later years, saw little traffic.

MERSTONE

Plate 135 From Horringford, the railway climbed the 1 in 440/54/140/70 incline of Redway Bank, curving on a 22 chain and then a 19 chain radius right-hand curve. After passing under Redway occupational bridge, the line entered the 301ft. long island platform at Merstone Junction, 5 miles 16 chains from Sandown. Originally, the station had a single platform but with the opening of the Newport, Godshill & St. Lawrence Railway in 1897, the station was rebuilt into an island by the IWCR. The station, half a mile south of the hamlet of Merstone, also served Rookley, 1½ miles to the west, but never generated much passenger traffic and was at it busiest when passengers interchanged between trains on the Ventnor and Sandown lines. This photograph shows Merstone Junction, facing Newport, in IWCR days, showing the large signal box, and beyond the level crossing, the pedestrian underpass originally built as access to and from the platform. The underpass often flooded as during wet weather, a brook, which flowed under the railway in an adjacent culvert, often rose in height and filled the tunnel with water. As rail traffic through Merstone was never heavy, the Southern Railway replaced the underpass with a pedestrian access ramp.

Plate 136 An 02 class 0-4-4T, No. W31 *Chale*, departs from Merstone with a Cowes to Sandown train in the summer of 1932. The distinctive route headcode, of one white disc or during darkness or fog or falling snow, one white headlamp over the left-hand buffer is carried by *Chale*. The train is an LSWR 3 set with a centre van brake third, a composite and an ex-PDSWJ brake third. Note the unmetalled road on the level crossing.

Plate 137 Merstone Junction Station, facing Newport, in 1929. In the foreground are the lines to Ventnor West (left) and Sandown (right).

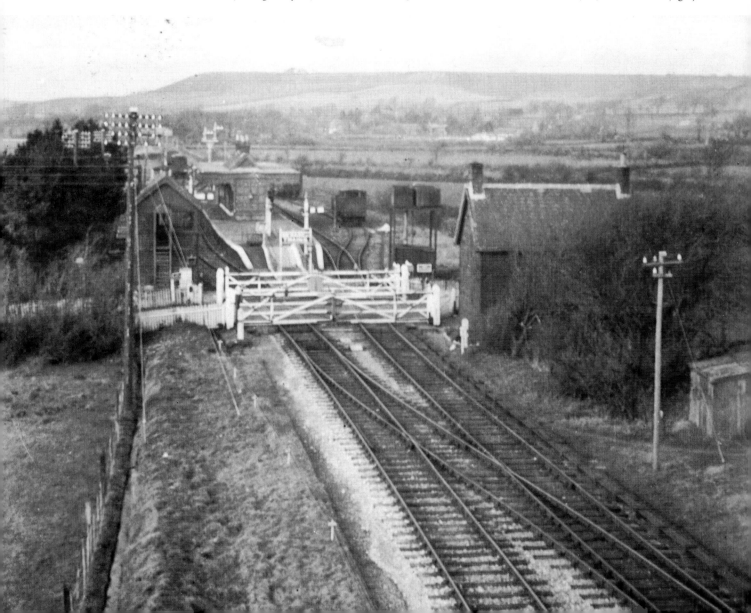

Plate 138 An 02 class 0-4-4T No. 20 *Shanklin* pulls into Merstone with a Sandown to Cowes train in 1949. *Shanklin* is in the early BR green livery.

Plate 139 Merstone Station, facing Newport, showing No. 1 siding, 360ft. in length, on the left of the main single line, used to stable Ventnor West trains. Coaching stock stands on No. 2 siding, which is 380ft. in length.

Plate 140 The engineer's end of No. 1 siding, and the 'down' platform road in a view facing Newport.

Plate 141 A busy scene at Merstone Junction on 3rd September 1952, with 02 class No. 27 *Merstone* on a Cowes to Sandown train on the left. No. W35 *Freshwater* awaits, on the right, with the connection to Ventnor West.

BLACKWATER

Plate 142 From Merstone, the railway joined the valley of the infant River Medina following a straight course falling at a gradient of 1 in 200/700/130 to Blackwater, 6 miles 77 chains from Sandown, and close to the roads connecting Shanklin and Sandown with Newport. This view, facing Newport, shows the original wooden platform on the west side of the line which was host to a wooden waiting shed.

Plate 143 The Southern Railway later rebuilt the platform to a length of 242ft. on the same site. No. 31 enters the new platform with a two coach train, shortly before the service was withdrawn in February 1956. The station house, adjacent to the level crossing, also contained the booking office.

SHIDE

Plate 144 Leaving Blackwater, the railway followed a fairly straight course, alongside the infant River Medina, falling at 1 in 300/230 to Shide Station, 8 miles 10 chains from Sandown on the southern extremity of the Island capital. Shide Station, located on an 8 chain radius curve, with its level crossing, facing Sandown, was a key token block post, splitting the section from Merstone to Newport South and is photographed in September 1920. The level crossing carried the Sandown to Newport road across the line.

Plate 145 Shide station building and small wooden signal box which housed a lever frame for operating the signals and points. Worthy of note is the distinctive nameboard, on the 173ft. long platform, and is located on the 'up' side of the line.

Plates 146 & 147 North of Shide, a siding left the branch, by trailing points on the 'up' side, to serve chalk and ballast pits under St. George's Down. The chalk was conveyed to Cement Mills beside the Medina, 1½ miles north of Newport on the Cowes line, whilst the ballast was utilized on the permanent way of the Island railway system. The upper photograph shows the chalk pit, whilst in the lower photograph, the fireman of 'Terrier' tank No. W8 *Freshwater* is climbing back into the cab after seeking authority for the train to enter the siding with empties from Cement Mills sidings. Because of the light flat-bottomed permanent way at both Cement Mills and Shide pits, the 'Terrier' tanks were the only locomotives permitted to work these services. Beyond Shide, the line continued on a 1 in 190 falling gradient before rising at 1 in 150 to Pan Lane Crossing. From the level crossing, falling gradients of 1 in 590/168 led to the junction south of Newport.

GODSHILL

Plates 148 & 149 From Merstone Junction, the erstwhile Newport, Godshill & St. Lawrence Railway, which was originally authorized in 1885 as the Shanklin & Chale Railway, ran south to serve a remotely-populated part of the Island. The line was a latecomer and was opened for traffic on 20th July 1897 to St. Lawrence, before ultimately terminating at Ventnor on 1st June 1900. After initially falling at a gradient of 1 in 300, the railway climbed at 1 in 116/130/180 to Godshill, 1 mile 48 chains from Merstone. Serving what is reputed to be the most attractive village in the Isle of Wight, the station was situated approximately half a mile to the west of the main centre of population, at the bottom of the hill in the shadow of the rather sinister-named Bleak Down. The IWCR always operated the line and the stations were substantially built. In the upper photograph the ornate oil lamps decorate the single platform, 300ft. in length, on the 'up' or east side of the line, In the lower photograph, little had altered by Southern Railway days, except for the substitution of the wooden nameboards by the ubiquitous ferro-concrete SR variety. Godshill handled daily milk traffic, and the churns on the platform are waiting to be loaded on to a Newport-bound train. Godshill was downgraded to an unstaffed halt in 1927. A 260ft. long siding to the east of the platform served the goods yard.

WHITWELL

Plate 150 Leaving Godshill, the branch climbed continuously, initially at 1 in 300/72/100 and finally for two miles at 1 in 72 to Whitwell, 4 miles 2 chains from Merstone. Originally built with a crossing loop, the station was located on the hillside above the village and served the catchment area of Niton, the Western Undercliff, Blackgang and Chale. The 'up' platform, 258ft. in length, was host to the booking office, waiting-rooms and station master's house whilst the slightly shorter 'down' platform boasted only a waiting shelter. A Ventnor Town to Merstone train, hauled by a 'Terrier' 0-6-0T, enters Whitwell soon after the opening of the line.

Plate 151 The NG & SLR was taken over by the IWCR in 1913 but, despite all efforts to attract passengers, the route to Ventnor by the IWR was always the more direct and more popular. When the Southern Railway took over the Island system in 1923, serious efforts were made to bring the railways up to a modern standard, and economies were made. The IWCR's route to Ventnor was an obvious choice for investigation, and in no way could the small amount of traffic justify the expense of the crossing loop at Whitwell. The loop was subsequently taken out of use in 1926 but remained in situ for over two years before its removal. This photograph, facing north, taken on 5th November 1928, shows the influence of the Southern Railway already in evidence, with the precast concrete nameboards and fencing posts. The signal box, soon to be removed, controlled the points to the 360ft. long siding on the 'up' side of the line.

ST. LAWRENCE

Plate 152 (above right) From Whitwell, the railway climbed at a gradient of 1 in 93 for three quarters of a mile to Dean Crossing, where the road from Whitwell to Ventnor bisected the line. The downs closed in as the railway entered St. Lawrence Tunnel (619 yds. long) and swept downhill at 1 in 55 to emerge on a 14 chain left-hand curve high above the undercliff, with breathtaking views, on the south side, of coastal scenery. This scene shows the south end of St. Lawrence Tunnel, and the adjacent footpath crossing, in 1920. The crossing was the scene of many near accidents as unsuspecting pedestrians were rudely awakened by trains charging towards them from the inky depths of the tunnel.

Plate 153 In April 1949, 'Terrier' tanks Nos. 8 and 13, which had worked the Merstone to Ventnor West motor trains, were returned to the mainland and replaced by two 02 class 0-4-4T locomotives, Nos. 35 and 36, which were fitted with motor gear. No. 36 *Carisbrooke* bursts out of St. Lawrence Tunnel with the branch push-pull train in 1950. Just discernible, above the arch of the tunnel, is the date of construction, 1897, which is carved in the stonework. The construction was a brick semicircular arch with a span diameter of 15ft. 8in.

Plate 154 The chalky embankment often caused problems along this section of line and, until the undergrowth had grown, cliff falls were common, especially after wet weather. In this scene a cliff fall, in 1903, opposite St. Lawrence Station, caused closure of the line for a day and permanent way staff who are attempting to clear the line are watched by local residents. The short siding, serving the small goods yard, can be seen just beyond the overbridge.

Plate 155 St. Lawrence Station, wedged between the downs and a public road, was located on a 1 in 160 falling gradient, 5 miles 44 chains from Merstone. The single platform, 220ft. in length, on the south side of the line, was the temporary terminus from 1897 until the extension to Ventnor Town was opened. St. Lawrence was downgraded to an unstaffed halt in 1927.

Plate 156 'Terrier' tanks were synonymous with the Ventnor Town (later Ventnor West) branch during the 55 year life of the line. In this view, IWCR No. 9 departs from St. Lawrence with a 'down' train in 1900, along the shelf on which the railway ran above the undercliff, shortly after the line had been extended to Ventnor. The leading vehicle is an ex-LSWR brake third. The roof destination boards on the coaching stock are of particular interest.

VENTNOR WEST

Plate 157 Ventnor Town Station, situated 6 miles 68 chains from Merstone, facing the buffer stops, in the early 1920s. Two platforms were provided, each 337ft. in length but the 'up' side, which was devoid of buildings saw very little use as most trains terminated on the 'down' side where facilities included booking office, waiting-room and refreshment room. Adjoining this building was the station master's house.

Plate 158 Unfortunately the IWCR station was over a mile west of the town centre and, on the takeover by the Southern Railway in 1923, they renamed the terminus, more appropriately, Ventnor West, altering, at the same time, the ex-IWR Ventnor Station to Ventnor Town. The exterior of Ventnor West, in the early 1930s, shows the fine single storey station buildings and, on the left, the two storey station master's house.

Plate 159 In IWCR days, in the early 1900s, Beyer Peacock 2-4-0T No. 5 stands at Ventnor Town with a train of three ex-IW(NJ)R 4 wheelers. The leading vehicle is first/second composite, IWCR No. 30, followed by a second/third class composite, IWCR No. 28 and two compartment brake third, No. 29. The coaches, originally built by the Bristol Carriage & Wagon Company, were subsequently rebuilt as vans.

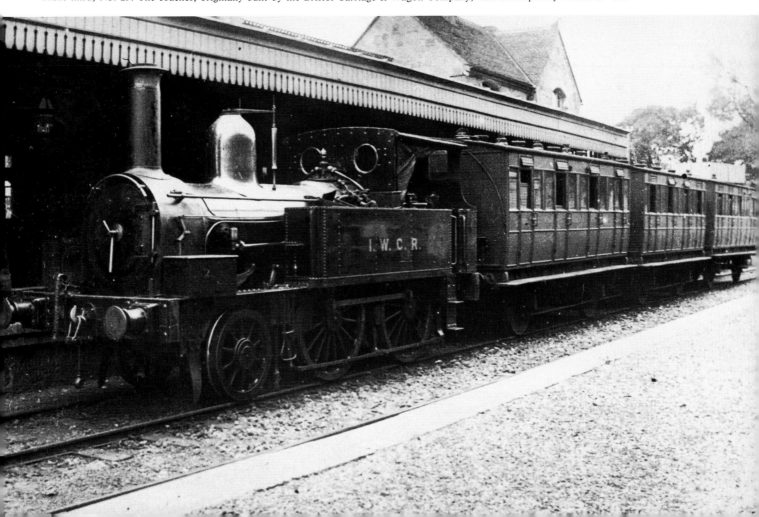

Plate 160 The ornate canopy and station buildings at Ventnor West, facing the buffer stops, showing the points to the run-round loop.

Plate 161 West of Ventnor West Station, points led to sidings in the picturesque and tree-lined ampitheatre. An 0-6-0T, No. W8 *Freshwater* approaches Ventnor West, in 1949, with a motor train from Merstone. In the foreground is the 60ft. long loop dock road with inspection pit and adjacent water tank and column. In the background, servicing the goods yard, is the 360ft. long Cliff siding and the 480ft. long coal road.

Plate 162 Motor train working was a feature of the Ventnor West branch for many years. Ex-LCDR 4 wheel push-pull set No. 483, formed of brake third No. 4111 and composite No. 6368, and set No. 484, brake third No. 4112 and composite No. 6369, sandwich 'Terrier' 0-6-0T No. 8 *Freshwater* at Ventnor West in 1936. With the introduction of these sets on the line, in 1924, conductor guard working was introduced, with the guard issuing tickets on the train. All station booking offices on the branch, other than at Ventnor West, were subsequently closed with the exception of Whitwell which opened during the summer season only. These push-pull sets were withdrawn in 1938. The destination board on the side of No. 4111 reads Merstone, St. Lawrence, Ventnor West.

Plate 163 Ventnor West, on 15th April 1950, with a 02 class 0-4-4T standing at the platform with single push-pull composite, No. 6987. After the closure of the Ventnor West line, on 15th September 1952, the single unit was used on the Bembridge branch prior to being withdrawn in December 1955. It was then broken up at St. Helen's Wharf. The appendage to the Southern Railway cast concrete station nameboard denotes that Ventnor West was 168ft. above sea level, 126ft. lower than the former IWR terminus.

NEWPORT (FYNR)

Plate 164 After the break with with IWCR, from 1st July 1913, the FYNR trains terminated and started from their own passenger station, which was sited south of the line, east of Hunny Hill footbridge. The simple timber platform was host to a wood and corrugated iron ticket office at the west end of the platform, with a signal box and waiting-room at the eastern end. The signal box controlled the run-round loop, signals and connection with the IWCR. There was an 'up' starting signal at the east end of the platform and 'up' home and 'down' starting signals on the same post west of the footbridge. This view shows the FYNR station, facing Freshwater, in 1920. This station was closed in the summer of 1923 and was later dismantled by the Southern Railway.

Plate 165 The FYNR goods yard at Newport was located west of the footbridge on the north side of the line, and was known, until closure, as the Freshwater yard. Entry from the main single line was controlled by a single lever ground frame, which was released by a key on the Newport to Carisbrooke (later Ningwood) token. The goods yard contained two goods sidings, a small carriage shed for the railcar and an engine shed. This view, facing Freshwater, taken in 1920, shows the entrance to the yard and the 'up' home and 'down' starter on the same post. Beyond the signal, on the curve, is the commencement of Hunny Hill Viaduct.

Plate 166 The FYNR Manning Wardle 0-6-0 saddle tank awaits departure from Newport on 12th May 1919 with a train composed of three ex-LSWR 4 wheel coaches and, behind the locomotive is, FYNR brake third, No. 9, an ex-NLR vehicle.

Plate 167 Beyond the goods yard, the FYNR crossed two bridges, known collectively as Newport Towngate or Hunny Hill Viaduct. The first was formed of nine 20ft. concrete arches, which were lined with brick and supported by brick piers, the arch increasing in height from 2ft. 10in. to 17ft. 6in. The second part was of wrought iron construction, with 19 girder spans resting on trestles. At 276ft. long the spans varied from 24ft. 9in. to 39ft. 9in. in length and the maximum height was 21ft. 2in. An 02 class locomotive, No. W30 *Shorwell*, crosses the second part of the viaduct, in 1935, with a Freshwater to Newport train, formed of two 4 wheel LCDR five compartment thirds, an LCDR close-coupled 4 set and a LSWR guard/luggage van.

Plate 168 The Southern Railway closed the FYNR station at Newport in the summer of 1923 and gradually demolished the platform and buildings. Remnants of the former station were still evident on 5th November 1928 when the former Freshwater 'Terrier', No. W2 passed the site of the platform whilst heading towards the junction at Newport North. In the background are the interchange sidings and carriage repair shops.

CARISBROOKE

Plate 169 From Newport, the railway climbed initially at a gradient of 1 in 60/110 before descending at 1 in 395. Continuing the climb at 1 in 67/95, the line entered Carisbrooke Station, 1 mile 21 chains from Newport. This 1920 photograph, facing west, shows the crossing loop disused. The Southern Railway later provided a concrete nameboard and single waiting shelter on the 'down' platform, 197 ft. in length. The 'up' platform was removed. The Southern Railway also removed the signals and provided location lights half a mile in each direction on the approach to the platform. Carisbrooke was downgraded to the status of a halt in 1927. Despite the attractions of the castle and church, few tourists used the station in later years, as it was half a mile north of the village and was only accessible by cart track.

Plate 170 A view of Carisbrooke Station and its overgrown goods yard, facing Newport, in 1949. The siding, 200ft. in length, ran through a gate and behind the 'down' platform. The yard was never extensively used although, during World War II, Parkhurst prisoners were employed in loading sugar beet into wagons.

GUNVILLE SIDING

Plate 171 Beyond Carisbrooke, the line climbed at a gradient of 1 in 66/395 to Gunville overbridge. A few chains beyond the bridge was Gunville siding, with accommodation for five wagons. This siding was located on the south side of the line with a connection facing 'down' trains. Situated on a 1 in 66 rising gradient in the 'down' direction, the siding served brickworks which produced not only bricks, but tiles and glazed pottery. The Southern Railway authorized traffic for the siding to be propelled from Newport, with a brake van as the leading vehicle, to enable the guard to hand-signal instructions to the driver.

WATCHINGWELL

Plate 172 From Gunville sidings, the line followed undulating gradients before descending at 1 in 66 to Upper Watchingwell Station, 3 miles 64 chains from Newport, where the 95ft. long platform was situated on the 'down', or south side, of the single line. Built for the private use of the owner of Swainstone Estate, 'his family, friends, tenants and persons having business with him,' the station was originally called Watchingwell. For many years, the name was omitted from public timetables and maps. The station also had a siding, 140ft. in length with access from the main single line, by points in a trailing connection, for 'down' trains.

Plate 173 Watchingwell Station, a view facing Newport. The station house was of a more recent construction than others on the FYNR. Originally two home signals shared the same post, being operated by a 2 lever ground frame on the platform. These signals were kept in the off position but were returned to danger when it was required to stop a train. The Southern Railway removed the siding and replaced the home signals by distant signals which were also returned to danger when it was required to stop a train.

CALBOURNE & SHALFLEET

Plate 174 On leaving Watchingwell, the FYNR followed a winding switchback route, falling at a gradient of 1 in 78, and then climbing at 1 in 78/64 before falling at 1 in 66, rising at 1 in 60 to Pound Lane level crossing. A short 1 in 66 falling gradient brought the line to Calbourne & Shalfleet Station, 5 miles 45 chains from Newport. Situated midway between the two villages, a mile to the south and north respectively, the station house was a simple single storey structure to which was added a waiting-room and booking office. In this scene, considerable activity is shown at Calbourne after the arrival of a Newport to Freshwater train, in September 1920.

Plate 175 When the Southern Railway assumed control of the line, the old wooden and corrugated iron ticket office, at Newport's FYNR station, was transferred to the eastern end of Calbourne platform to act as a booking office. At the same time, in 1925, the primitive signal box which controlled distant home and starting signals in each direction, was abolished and was replaced by two ground frames. The block instrument was transferred to the new booking office whilst the west frame controlled entry to the 160ft. single line siding. The eastern frame on the platform, outside the booking office, controlled the 'up' and 'down' home signals and the gate lock. The distant signals became fixed and the starting signals were removed.

Plate 176 Calbourne & Shalfleet Station from the west, with wagons in the single line siding of the goods yard, which was served by trailing points from the main single line in the 'down' direction.

Plate 177 From Calbourne, the railway descended initially at a gradient of 1 in 111 and then at 1 in 68 to Calbourne Viaduct (bridge No. 16), a trestle bridge 237ft. in length. It was made up of nine spans, varying from 23ft. to 27ft. 6in., with a maximum height of 23ft. 8in. above the waters of the Caul Bourne, a tributary of the Newtown River. An 02 class locomotive, No. 27 *Merstone*, crosses the viaduct on 26th September 1952 with the two coach 2.40p.m. Newport to Freshwater train.

NINGWOOD

Plate 178 Away from Calbourne Viaduct the railway climbed steeply out of the valley of the Caul Bourne at 1 in 57 before descending at 1 in 80/100/200/70 to Ningwood Station, situated 6 miles 77 chains from Newport, with its passing loop. The driver of IWCR Beyer Peacock 2-4-0T No. 4 is giving attention to his locomotive, which is standing at Ningwood with a Newport to Freshwater train, in the early 1900s. The IWCR, when working the Freshwater line, made no special allocation of motive power or coaching stock, although the use of the 45 ton locomotive No. 2, and the 40 ton locomotive No. 6, was frowned upon, and finally, in 1912, was prohibited. The Southern Railway later banned the 02 class 0-4-4T locomotives from the line until the permanent way had been relaid and the bridges had been strengthened. The coaching stock is of early LSWR vintage, a 4 wheel four compartment composite, a five compartment 4 wheel third, a 4 wheel four compartment composite and a two compartment brake third.

Plate 179 Ningwood Station and crossing loop, facing Freshwater. The Southern Railway extended the loop to a length of 400ft., to accommodate longer trains, and provided the water tank on the Newport end of the 216ft. long 'up' platform for the replenishment of locomotives. In 1927, the Southern Railway also introduced modifications to the signalling arrangements which allowed Ningwood signal box to be closed when traffic was light. Two short section staffs, Newport to Ningwood and Ningwood to Freshwater, were used when the signal box was open and one long section staff, Newport to Freshwater, when the box was closed.

Plate 180 An 02 class 0-4-4T, No. 34 *Newport*, leaves Ningwood for Yarmouth in 1948. The points to the goods yard siding, shown in advance of the train, were operated by a 2 lever ground frame, which was released by a key attached to the train staff.

Plate 181 An 02 class 0-4-4T pulls into Ningwood with a Newport to Freshwater train. The station master's house is in the left background and the signal box is in the foreground on the 216ft. long 'down' platform.

YARMOUTH

Plate 182 Beyond Ningwood, a climb at 1 in 78/55 brought the line to a minor summit. Following undulating gradients, including a long descent at 1 in 64, the railway curved around 19 and 38 chain left-hand curves to Yarmouth. Yarmouth Station, 9 miles 78 chains from Newport, was situated at the back of the ancient town, and half a mile from the pier and the slipway. The layout was unusual in that the platforms were staggered. The main station buildings were on the 'up' platform whilst the 'down' platform was host to a small waiting shelter. In this photograph, taken in 1920, the 'down' loop is disused although the signal box, which controls signals and points to the goods yard, remains in use at the eastern end of the 'up' platform. Next to the signal box is a haystack which is evidently owned by the FYNR.

Plate 183 Twenty five years or so later, the scene has changed considerably, as the former 'down' platform and waiting shelter stand forlornly isolated. On the 177ft. long 'up' platform, the oil lamps have given way to gas lamp standards, whilst flat-bottomed track has been replaced by bullhead track. In the background, the points from the main single line led to the 320ft. long siding on the 'up' side of the line.

Plate 184   A view looking west from Yarmouth Station with the railway running alongside the small embankment on a 17 chain radius curve, above the open and exposed mudflats situated beside the Western Yar.

Plate 185   Yarmouth Station from the west. The platform layout of the station was staggered due to the stream which passed beneath the line near the end of the 'up' side platform, necessitating the provision of an underbridge (No. 25). An 02 class 0-4-4T, No. 29 *Alverstone*, carrying the wrong headcode, prepares to depart with the 3 coach 12.40p.m. Newport to Freshwater train, on 18th September 1953.

FRESHWATER

Plate 186 Freshwater Station was the largest on the erstwhile FYNR. The frontage of the two storey red brick building suggested a medium-sized terminus, but only a single narrow platform was provided on the 'up' side of the line. The platform was originally very short and was lengthened several times. This view, facing the buffer stops, in September 1920, shows the run-round loop, two of the three goods sidings and the short cattle dock siding.

Plate 187 Considerable improvements and alterations were made by the Southern Railway in 1927, when the old engine shed and carriage sheds were pulled down and the sidings and end dock were removed. The station office accommodation was increased and the concourse near the buffer stops was enlarged. The single platform was also partly rebuilt and extended and was backed by standard SR pre-stressed concrete fencing units. At the same time, the old signal box was replaced by the one which was formerly located at Newport (FYNR) and was sited by the concourse, behind the buffer stops of the dock road, to enable the porter/signalman to assist with station duties. The new platform can be seen in this 1927 view of 'Terrier' No. W11 waiting to depart with a Newport train.

Plate 188 The Southern Railway added further improvements at Freshwater in 1932 when the platform was again extended to accommodate the newly-introduced 6 coach 'Tourist' trains, which ran from Shanklin and Sandown through to Yarmouth and Freshwater. An 02 class locomotive, No. 29 *Alverstone*, stands at the head of a three coach train, at the extended platform, in September 1953.

Plate 189 Although the Southern Railway, which was formed on 1st January 1923, absorbed the IWR and IWCR from that date, the FYNR disputed the terms and stayed nominally independent until 1st August 1923. FYNR 'Terrier' No. 2, still in independent livery and fitted with vacuum brake and Drummond boiler, blackens the landscape as she shunts out her train at Freshwater on 11th June 1923. Behind the locomotive is the engine shed and water tank and, to the right, with IWR open wagon No. 100 standing alongside, is the goods shed.

Plate 190 From Causeway Crossing the FYNR descended at a gradient of 1 in 500/1000, round a 22 chain radius right-hand curve, across marshland and the upper reaches of the river, to Freshwater Station, situated 11 miles 78 chains from Newport. In early Southern Railway's days, A1 class 0-6-0T 'Terrier' No. 9 enters the station with a train from Newport. The 4 wheel coaches are believed to be from set No. 493 and include ex-MSLR, FYNR No. 1, SR No. 6990, a GER five compartment third, SR No. 2445, and another MSLR vehicle. On the right, LBSCR 10 ton open wagon, No. 26145 retains its raised round ends. The old FYNR signal box can be seen to the left of the starting signal.

Plate 191 A 'Terrier' 0-6-0 tank No. 9 *Fishbourne* stands off the end of the platform at Freshwater waiting to depart for Newport with ex-LBSCR Billinton close-coupled 4 wheel set No. 497. After the Grouping, the 'Terriers' soon replaced the FYNR and former IWCR locomotives on the line and one of the locomotives was rostered to run 150 or so miles a day on Freshwater branch diagrams. The 'Terriers' were taxed, however, by heavy trains and, for a short period betwen 1931 and 1933, were replaced by the ex-IWR locomotives No. 13 *Ryde* and No. 16 *Wroxall*. When the 2-4-0T succumbed to the cutters' torch, the 'Terriers' continued working the services but lost most duties when replaced by the 02 class locomotives in 1936. Three sets of the Billinton close-coupled coaches were used on the Island. Set No. 497 was formed of brake thirds Nos. 4113 and 4114, composite No. 6370 and five compartment third No. 2343.

Plate 192 An earlier view shows the older FYNR station nameboard with Freshwater advertised 'for Totland Bay and Freshwater Bay'. Ex-IWCR Beyer Peacock 2-4-0T No. 8, built in 1898, stands waiting to run round the LBSCR stock which it has hauled from Newport. The light flat-bottomed track is still in place and was replaced by bullhead track in 1926, two years after this photograph was taken.

Plate 193 The station nameboard displays 'Freshwater for Alum Bay and Totland Bay' as ex-FYNR 'Terrier' 0-6-0T No. W2 *Freshwater* draws to a stop near the buffers on 3rd November 1928. The train is formed of four 4 wheel Stroudley-designed close-coupled set of London, Brighton & South Coast Railway stock.

Plate 194 Locomotives usually worked boiler first to Freshwater but there were exceptions in Southern Railway days when the 02 class locomotives were used on all routes. An 02 class 0-4-4T No. 29 *Alverstone* awaits departure from Freshwater, on 6th September 1937, with a six coach through train to Ryde. In accordance with the SR route headcode used on the Isle of Wight, No. 29 is carrying the disc at the base of the chimney; the code for the Freshwater line. Ironically, this was also the code for Ryde Pierhead to Ventnor.

Plate 195 The station entrance had changed very little when the Southern Railway took over control and, except for the large notice 'Freshwater Station', the only change is the modified awning above the booking office entrance and the ordinary gas lamp in place of the ornate lantern. The entrance road has also been tarmacked.

NEWPORT SHED

Plate 196   The Isle of Wight Central Railway built their shed at Newport in the late 1870s. It was constructed of wood, with pitched corrugated sheeting on the roof, which had a central raised vent. The shed was host to two roads, designated No. 1 and No. 2 shed roads. It was a through building and, at the north end, a cast-iron water tank was located above No. 2 road. An 02 class 0-4-4T, No. 30, and an unidentified 'Terrier' stand outside the shed in 1930.

Plate 197   The IWCR provided a locomotive repair shop at Newport but it was also used to repair coaching stock and wagons. By the late 1920s, the Southern Railway had transferred all locomotive repair work to their ex-IWR establishment at Ryde and, subsequently, from 1929, the shop was utilized for carriage painting, being converted at a cost of £423. This 1912 view shows IWCR 0-4-4T No. 2 stripped of its cab, standing in the north end doorway of the engine repair shop.

RYDE SHED

Plate 198 The initial engine shed, provided by the IWR at Ryde, was a two road structure, built of brick, which was later incorporated into the Works. Four locomotives could be accommodated but, with the increase in stock it became necessary to provide a larger shed. The only suitable site was to the west of the goods yard and, in 1872, a new shed was built by Morton & Co. of Liverpool on foundations provided by the IWR, although it was not used to stable engines until 1874. The two road double-ended structure, built of corrugated iron, was provided with inspection pits and the siding alongside served a covered coal stage. The shed, which accommodated six engines, three on each road, is shown looking from the south.

Plate 199 By the late 1920s, the situation of the engine shed in the middle of the goods yard, proved to be an operational nuisance. The Southern Railway duly built a new shed on the west side of St. John's Road Station and this modern structure was opened in May 1930. The two road single-ended building accommodated eight 02 class tank engines and included, in its construction, the use of steel lattice girders, previously used as support gantries for overhead wires on the LBSCR lines in South London.

LOCOMOTIVES (FYNR)

Plate 200 Freshwater, Yarmouth & Newport Railway locomotive No. 1 was a standard Manning Wardle Q class 0-6-0 saddle tank (maker's No. 1555). It was built in February 1902, and employed by Pauling & Company as No. 56 *Northolt*, on the construction of the Great Western and Great Central Joint line between Northolt Junction and High Wycombe. Purchased in June 1913 for £725, No. 1 was repainted in emerald green with bright red lining before entering service with the FYNR. No. 1 is pictured at Newport, in 1919.

Plate 201 Under the Southern Railway, FYNR No. 1 became No. W1 and had its vacuum brakes replaced by the Westinghouse brake in May 1924. After the transfer of 'Terrier' No. W10 to the Freshwater line, No. W1 was used on shunting duties and freight trip workings between Medina Wharf and Newport. No. 1 received the name *Medina* and is shown in Southern Railway livery at Newport in June 1931.

Plate 202 FYNR locomotive No. 2 was a Stroudley 'Terrier' 0-6-0T, which was built at Brighton in December 1876 as No. 46 *Newington*. It was later purchased by the London & South Western Railway in March 1903 for the Lyme Regis branch. It was renumbered 734 and was provided with a Drummond pattern boiler at Eastleigh Works in September 1912. After the break with the IWCR, the FYNR was desperate for motive power and, when the LSWR offered the loan of No. 734 at 15 shillings per day plus shipment costs, with the option to purchase it for £900 in the following spring, the offer was accepted. The 'Terrier' entered service with the FYNR on 1st July 1913 and was finally purchased in March 1914 with payment spread over three years.

LOCOMOTIVES (IWCR)

Plate 203 Isle of Wight Central Railway 2-2-2WT No. 1 *Pioneer* at Newport. Together with No. 2 *Precursor*, the pair formed the initial motive power for the Cowes & Newport Railway. At first, they were not owned by the Company but were the property of, and worked under contract by H. D. Martin, the contractor. Built by Slaughter, Gruning & Co. (maker's Nos. 453 and 454) in January 1862, they were employed during the construction of the line and were painted bright blue with red lining. After the July 1887 amalgamation of the C & N, R & N and IW(NJ) railways, the pair were numbered 1 and 2 in the IWCR fleet and painted in a dull red, with numbers substituted for names. No. 2 was withdrawn in January 1900 and No. 1 in August 1901. Both were broken up in October 1901.

Plate 204 H. D. Martin purchased a third locomotive for the C & NR from Black Hawthorn & Co. for £1,385 in February 1870. Named *Mill Hill*, it was a small 0-4-2ST and was initially painted in a dull olive green with white lining. Later, this locomotive was regularly employed shunting at Medina Wharf and was nicknamed *The Snatcher*. In 1908, No. 3 was reconstructed with a cased-in boiler and cab and attached to an ex-Midland Railway 12 wheel coach. As railcar No. 2, it entered traffic in its new guise on 18th April 1909 working on the Freshwater and Ventnor line. The railcar was laid aside in May 1913 when the coach was removed, after which time the locomotive was used at Medina Wharf for a few months before being placed in store at Newport. On 14th February 1918, together with the locomotive off railcar No. 1, No. 3 was sold to Holloway Brothers, London for the sum of £750, later working at Furness Withy Docks, Middlesbrough and later it was resold to William Benson & Son Ltd., Fourstone Quay, Hexham. No. 3 is shown here at Newport.

Plate 205 IWCR Beyer Peacock 2-4-0T No. 4, originally R & N Railway *Cowes*, receives attention from her driver at Newport in 1909, before departing for Cowes. No. 4 was finally withdrawn by the Southern Railway in September 1925.

Plate 206 This locomotive was the sister engine to No. 4, and originally named *Osborne*. It was built for the R & NR by Beyer Peacock (maker's No. 1584) in May 1876. Numbered 5 by the IWCR, it is shown at Freshwater still bearing the name *Osborne*. No. 5 was withdrawn from traffic in April 1926.

Plate 207 IWCR No. 7 was acquired from the North London Railway in 1880 at a price of £800. Built in October 1861 by Slaughter, Gruning & Co., this 4-4-0T was numbered 35A and was delivered to the Isle of Wight in full NLR livery. It was thought to have been named *Whippingham* by the C & N and R & N Joint Committee, but the IWCR numbered it 7 in July 1887. The 4-4-0 was placed in store, in 1906, and it was broken up by a local firm of scrap merchants on Medina Wharf in January/February 1907. No. 7 is pictured at Freshwater, whilst working on FYNR service, at the turn of the century.

Plate 208   IWCR No. 6 was a robust 4-4-0T with outside cylinders which was built by Black Hawthorn & Co., of Gateshead, (maker's No. 999) and delivered to the Island in June 1890. It was the first of the Company's locomotives to be fitted with the Westinghouse brake and the locomotive cost £1,845. After the Grouping, the Southern Railway transferred No. 6 to Ryde Shed, with the intention of using it on Ryde to Ventnor trains, but this proved to be an unpopular move, and it spent most of the time out of traffic before being withdrawn in September 1925. No. 6 had the distinction of being the only 4-4-0 tank engine which was taken into Southern Railway stock.

Plate 209   The IWCR were very satisfied with the performance of Nos. 4 and 5 and, in 1896, requested Beyer Peacock & Co. to quote for the construction of another 2-4-0T. Owing to full order books, delivery was delayed until 29th May 1898 and the new locomotive, No. 8 (maker's No. 3942), costing £1,950, entered service on 1st June. Shown here in SR livery at Newport, No. 8 was finally withdrawn from traffic in November 1929.

Plate 210 IWCR 'Terrier' 0-6-0T No. 9, pictured at Newport. Formerly LBSCR No. 75 *Blackwall*, it was purchased in March 1899, payment being made under a hire-purchase agreement with the Southern Counties Rolling Stock Finance Company, who paid the mainland railway and received, in return, a monthly payment from the IWCR of £9 8s 10d. The locomotive retained its original A1 boiler but received the usual Island extended bunker. Its service in Southern Railway livery was short lived for, during the evening of 28th March 1926, it sustained collision damage and was officially withdrawn from traffic the following month, being sold for scrap in April 1927.

Plate 211 Ex-IWCR 'Terrier' No. 10 *Cowes* pictured at Newport Shed in 1930. At the end of the nineteenth century, the IWCR was desperate for motive power, to replace ageing stock and, on 20th December 1899, they again approached the LBSCR for a six-coupled tank locomotive. The mainland company subsequently offered 'Terrier' 0-6-0T No. 69 *Peckham,* at a price of £700, and after Dugald Drummond, of the LSWR, had inspected the locomotive at Brighton Shed, he recommended purchase. The locomotive arrived in the Isle of Wight on 18th April 1900 and after general repair and repainting, emerged as IWCR No. 10. In common with other IWCR 'Terriers', No. 10 was fitted with a cast-iron chimney which was made by the Newport foundry of Wheeler & Hurst, and an extended coal bunker to the rear of the frames, which increased the capacity to 1½ tons. No. 10 entered service with the Southern Railway from January 1923 and was rebuilt to A1X class and named *Cowes*. It was fitted with a Marsh pattern chimney in place of the locally-cast one in April 1930. No. W10 returned to the mainland in May 1936 after the arrival of the larger 02 class locomotives and was stored in Eastleigh paint shops to await a decision as to its future, until October 1940. Together with No. W12, it was relegated to the Works dump and slowly rusted away before being broken up at the end of March 1949.

Plate 212   The most famous of the IWCR 'Terrier' acquisitions from the LBSCR was No. 11. Originally No. 40 *Brighton*, on the mainland system, and built in March 1878, she later became surplus to requirements, and was bought at a price of £600 in November 1901 and was transferred to the Island on 8th January 1902. No. 11 shown in original A1 class condition, with small bunker and LBSCR chimney, stands in the 'up' platform at Newport. The locomotive was later rebuilt with a cast-iron chimney from the Newport foundry of Wheeler & Hurst, and received extension of the coal bunker to the rear of the frames. In addition, in May 1918, it was provided with a new LBSCR AIX class boiler, with circular smokebox.

Plate 213   Durings its early Southern Railway career, No. 11 was utilized on the Brading to Bembridge branch and was allocated to Ryde Shed, where it is pictured on No. 3 shed road on 31st May 1930. Later named *Newport* it subsequently returned to Newport Shed to work the Merstone to Ventnor West services, the Shide to Cement Mills cement trains, as well as shunting Medina Wharf. Together with No. 8 and No. 13, *Newport* was later fitted with motor train gear for Ventnor West push-pull services. No. 11 was returned to the mainland in February 1947, renumbered 2640 and later 32640, being replaced by 02 class No. W34, which assumed the name *Newport*. The 'Terrier' worked the Hayling Island services until it was condemned in September 1963. After exhibition at Pwllheli Holiday Camp for some years, it has now returned to the Isle of Wight Steam Railway for further service on familiar metals.

Plate 214   Ex-IWCR 'Terrier' No. 12 *Ventnor*, originally LBSCR No. 84 *Crowborough*, purchased in November 1903 for £700, is shown as running in Southern Railway pre-war livery with the nameplate on the tank side. This locomotive returned to the mainland in May 1936 when the name was transferred to 02 class 0-4-4T No. 16.

Plate 215   By November 1905, the old North London 4-4-0T No. 7 was regularly out of traffic and caused serious inconvenience to the operating of train services on the IWCR. After a fruitless search, a replacement was found, in November 1906, when the Midland & South Western Junction Railway agreed to sell their Beyer Peacock 2-4-0T No. 6, dating from 1882, for £695. Unfortunately, the locomotive had been out of use for five months and required heavy repairs before it was accepted by the IWCR authorities. Allotted the number 7, on the IWCR, the 2-4-0T was well-suited to the Company's requirements and cost little on maintenance. Early in 1920 it received extensive overhaul in Newport Works when ageing balance safety valves were removed from the dome and replaced by a pair of Ramsbottom valves which were fitted over the firebox. The elegant copper-capped chimney was also replaced by the IWCR pattern cast-iron chimney from Wheeler & Hurst's foundry. No. 7 is shown at Sandown, in her original condition.

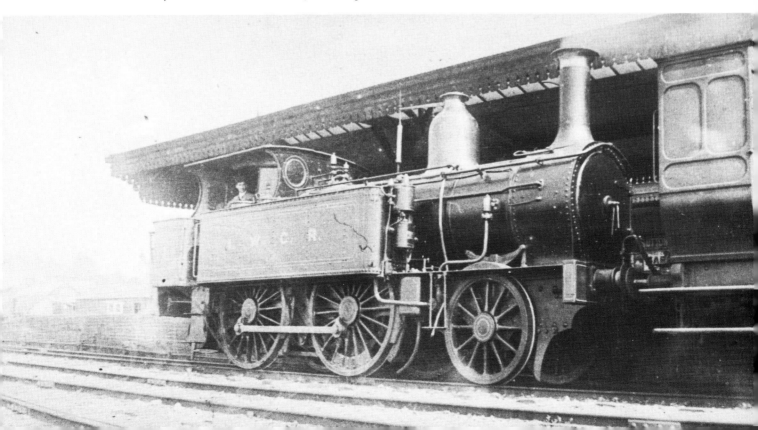

LOCOMOTIVES (IWR)

Plates 216 & 217 Initially, the Directors of the Isle of Wight Railway thought that two locomotives would suffice for the opening of their line from Ryde to Shanklin. After much argument, the number was increased to three and these locomotives were subsequently ordered at a cost of £2,250 each from Beyer Peacock & Co. Delivery of the trio took place on 22nd July 1864, ready for the opening of the railway on 23rd August. The three locomotives, weighing 30 tons 8½ cwt. each, were of standard Beyer Peacock design, and were originally fitted with elegant copper-capped chimneys and large brass domes over their flush-topped fireboxes. These initial locomotives were named *Ryde,* (maker's No. 400) *Sandown,* (maker's No. 401) and *Shanklin* (maker's No. 402). *Ryde,* which hauled the first public passenger train to Shanklin, received numerous modifications over the years and was numbered W13 by the Southern Railway in 1923. After withdrawal, on 2nd July 1932, with a total mileage of 1,556,846, it was stored under cover in the running shed at Ryde, where various old fittings were added, including cab and chimney. It was then repainted in grey with black and white livery in IWR style (upper photograph), and efforts were made to permanently preserve it. In June 1934, it was transferred to Eastleigh paint shops but money was scarce and this famous locomotive was finally broken up in August 1940. The lower photograph shows *Ryde* as SR No. W13, standing alongside the original shed at Ryde.

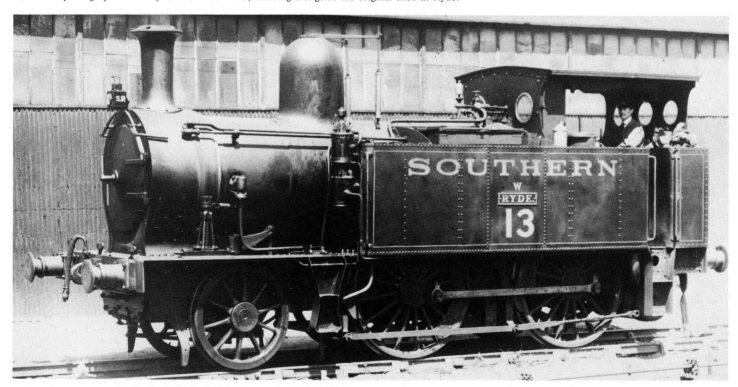

Plate 218 *Shanklin* was the third of the trio of Beyer Peacock tanks initially named by the IWR. Because of damage sustained whilst hauling a ballast train, it did not work on the official opening day of the line from Ryde to Shanklin. *Shanklin* outlived sister locomotive *Sandown,* to enter Southern Railway stock as No. W14, and is shown in SR livery outside the former IWR shed at Ryde in 1927, shortly before withdrawal in November of that year. Her final mileage was a creditable 1,492,121.

Plate 219 By 1868, with their finances greatly improved and traffic increasing, the IWR Directors placed an order with Beyer Peacock for another 2-4-0T locomotive. Costing £2,250 and named *Ventnor* (maker's No. 848) it was delivered in August 1868. Like its sister locomotives, *Ventnor* had no cab and the footplate was open to the elements. Between 1882 and 1884, all four locomotives were provided with a square-shaped cab and the chimneys were shortened by some three inches. *Ventnor*, later renumbered W15 by the Southern Railway, before condemnation in September 1925, is shown taking water at Ventnor in 1892. The photograph gives a good indication of the IWR Furness Red livery with black lining of the period. The small turntable used to enable locomotives to run round their trains is also of interest.

Plate 220 As traffic on the IWR increased, so the need for further locomotives became increasingly evident and in January 1871, Beyer Peacock & Co. were requested to supply a fifth locomotive to the Company. After lengthy legal wrangling regarding method of payment, *Wroxall* (maker's No. 1141), a 2-4-0T weighing 31 tons 14 cwt., was delivered on 10th April 1872 at a cost of £2,390. The locomotive differed from the other four by having the dome and Salter balance safety valves on the middle rung of the boiler. *Wroxall* survived to become No. W16 in Southern Railway's days and continued to give good service with its new owner. At the end of 1930, it was taken into Ryde Works, where it received second-hand cylinders, the cab of ex-IWCR 2-4-0T No. 8, a Drummond pattern chimney, standard SR nameplates and new tank side sheets. After running in from Ryde Shed, *Wroxall* was transferred to Newport and worked the Freshwater services until withdrawn from traffic in July 1933, with a total mileage of 1,350,674. No. W16 *Wroxall* is shown here in ex-Works condition after the rebuilding, early in 1931.

Plate 221 Up to the mid-1870s, the IWR had adequate locomotive power for the increasing summer traffic, whilst winter services could be handled by three engines, leaving two available for maintenance or works repair. In 1876, a further 2-4-0T was ordered from Beyer Peacock & Co. of Manchester and was delivered to the Island on 6th December 1876. Named *Brading* (maker's No. 1638), and weighing 34 tons 8cwt., it did not enter service until 4th March 1877, and is shown standing at Ryde Pierhead in 1915. The locomotive was numbered W17 by the Southern Railway, but was condemned in April 1926 after completing 1,212,753 miles.

Plates 222 & 223 The last engine which was purchased by the IWR was *Bonchurch* (maker's No. 2376), a more powerful machine than previously supplied by Beyer Peacock & Co. Ordered on 16th October 1882, at a cost of £2,100, and required for the summer service of the following year, delivery was due on 30th April 1883, but the barge conveying the locomotive across The Solent foundered in sheltered and shallow water off Bembridge. Salvage operations were quickly organized and *Bonchurch* was dragged along the sea bed into St. Helen's where it was returned to dry land by means of rails which were laid at low tide and with assistance given by the locomotive *Bembridge* and sheerlegs. Little damage was sustained and, after attention at Ryde Works, this 35 ton 14½cwt. 2-4-0T locomotive entered service for the summer traffic. *Bonchurch*, shown in Ryde yard, differed from the other Beyer Peacock tanks in having cab sides and a rear bunker. Because of the bunker it was unable to use the Bembridge turntable and, therefore, never worked the branch passenger services. Numbered by the Southern Railway W18, (see below), it was withdrawn in May 1928 after completing 1,326,067 miles on the Island, latterly for freight and for station pilot duties at Newport.

Plate 224 (top left) *Bembridge*, a Manning Wardle M class 0-6-0ST, was acquired by the IWR on 2nd August 1898, although it was used by the Company from 27th May 1882 when traffic commenced on the Bembridge branch. Originally named *Stanley*, the saddle tank was delivered in March 1875 to Scott & Edwards of Melmerby, who built the branch for the Brading Harbour Improvement & Railway Co. On completion of the contract, the locomotive was sold for £650 and during 1903, it took part in trials for oil firing, being used initially on the Bembridge branch and then by the IWCR before the equipment was removed on 16th October. *Bembridge* spent considerable time in store during World War I and when a letter, dated 26th April 1916, was received from the Inspector of Iron Structures, War Office, requesting surplus locomotives for the war effort, the engine was offered at a cost of £750. This proved acceptable and it left the Island in June 1916. It is shown in its original style.

Plate 225 (bottom left) *Bembridge* at Brading on the branch train in 1912, with the rather ugly storepipe chimney which had been fitted in the previous year.

LOCOMOTIVES (SOUTHERN RAILWAY)

Plates 226 (above), 227 & 228 (overleaf) In 1932, a new quay was under construction at Medina Wharf and the new structure was capable of bearing the weight of heavier locomotives. The Southern Railway took the opportunity to replace some of the 'Terrier' tanks with the larger ex-LBSCR E1 class 0-6-0T locomotives. Nos. B136, B152 and B154 were taken to Eastleigh Works and fitted with Marsh type boilers, and had condensing gear feed pumps and vacuum ejectors removed before being repainted in green and being renumbered as W1 *Medina*, W2 *Yarmouth* and W3 *Ryde* respectively. The trio were transferred to the Island in July 1932 and immediately set to work on the coal trains between Medina Wharf and Newport. These coal trains had been restricted to 25 loaded wagons but soon the E1 class locomotives were handling trains of 40 loaded wagons, with 45 empties being worked back to the Wharf. So successful were the class that a fourth locomotive, ex-No. B131, was modified and transferred to the Island as No. W4 *Wroxall*, in July 1933. Later, the E1 class locomotives proved equally successful in hauling passenger services and were regularly diagrammed for the heavy 'Tourist Express' between Ventnor and Newport and return, and also between Ryde Pierhead and Ventnor. In these views, No. 2 *Yarmouth* is shown at Newport after arriving with a train of coal wagons from Medina Wharf whilst No. 3 *Ryde* stands in Ryde Shed. The front view of No. 3 shows the high cleaning standard given to the Island locomotives in the mid-1930s. The ornate star, around the smokebox door handle, is another embellishment, reminiscent of Island practice. With the demise of goods traffic on the Isle of Wight system after World War II, all four locomotives were quickly withdrawn; No. 2 in August 1956, No. 1 in March 1957, No. 3 in June 1959 and No. 4 in October 1960.

Plates 229 & 230 (top right & bottom right) At the Grouping, the newly-formed Southern Railway found the need on the Island for more modern motive power. During the holiday periods, there were few locomotives in sound condition to haul the services. On the South Western Section of the Southern Railway, a number of Adams 02 class 0-4-4 tank engines were surplus to requirements and so, to ease the position, two of the class, ex-LSWR Nos. 206 and 211, were transferred to the Island via Ryde Pier in May 1923. So successful were the class that a further twenty one were transferred between 1924 and 1949. No. 188 was one of four 02 class locomotives transferred to the Island in April 1925, via Medina Wharf, and is shown at Ryde in June 1926, as No. W23, with large numerals on the side tank, the original small bunker with coal rails, Westinghouse pump adjacent to the left-hand side of the smokebox, and air reservoir on top of the left-hand side tank. The following year, No. W28 (ex-No. 186) was transferred to the Island. This locomotive, akin with Nos. W27 and W29 to W32, was delivered carrying the new Drummond pattern boiler with dome top lock-up safety valve. All suffered from erratic steaming and priming, and were shedded at Newport where duties, carried out by 02 class locomotives, were considered lighter than their counterparts at Ryde. No. 28 is shown at Newport Shed in June 1926.

Plate 231 (top left) The 02 class locomotives remained nameless until October 1928, when nameplates of local origin were cast at Eastleigh Works and sent to the Isle of Wight for mounting on the tank sides. The fitting of the nameplates necessitated the resiting of the locomotive number from the side tanks to the bunker. The 'W' prefix remained until 1931 after which it only appeared on the cast brass numberplates bolted to the bunker back plates. No. 30 *Shorwell* stands at Ryde Shed and is seen after being fitted with nameplates.

Plates 232 (bottom left), 233 & 234 These three photographs show No. W22 *Brading* and No. W24 *Calbourne* at Ryde Shed, in 1930, and No. W27 *Merstone* at Newport, the latter being fitted with the Drummond type boiler. The immaculate condition of the engines and the star embellishment on the smokebox of No. 22 is worthy of note. No. W27 differs from Nos. W22 and W24 in having flush type coupling rods instead of the fluted type, and No. W27 was also the only 02 class locomotive to have four rails on the bunker instead of the usual three. *Merstone* is also fitted with a hooter, instead of a whistle.

Plates 235, 236 & 237 In the early 1930s, the popularity of the Isle of Wight brought an ever increasing number of visitors to the eastern resorts of Sandown, Shanklin and Ventnor. So well patronized were the trains, that the Southern Railway decided to increase the Saturday service from Ryde Pierhead for the 1933 season by providing three trains to Ventnor, one to Sandown and one to Cowes each hour between 10a.m. and 6p.m. Unfortunately, the number of locomotives required for the new service rendered costs prohibitive, as engines were required all too often to run light from Ryde Pierhead to Ryde St. John's for coaling, halfway through their diagram. A. B. MacLeod, who was assistant for the Island, was given the task of finding a solution, and with Bob Sweetman, his Works foreman at Ryde, devised ways and means of cutting down the light running, by increasing the bunker capacity of the 02 class locomotives. Initially, additional coal rails were suggested but these proved to be impractical. A

high solid-sided bunker was then tried on No. W19 *Osborne* but, during August 1932, locomotive crews complained that the view through the rear cab spectacles was restricted, as to be dangerous, especially in windy weather. The next experiment involved a bunker bowing out over the rear buffer beam similar to the Z class 0-8-0T locomotives. By lowering the height of the bunker to the base level of the spectacle plate, this arrangement proved satisfactory and No. W26 *Whitwell* was so fitted, in September 1932. The bunker capacity was doubled from 1½ tons to 3 tons and became standard in the 02 class locomotives. No. 19 was subsequently returned to the Works for the new standard bunker to be fitted. No. 19 is seen with the original bunker (top picture) and the first experimental bunker (centre picture). No. W26 has the new standard bunker (bottom picture). All are seen at Ryde St. John's Road.

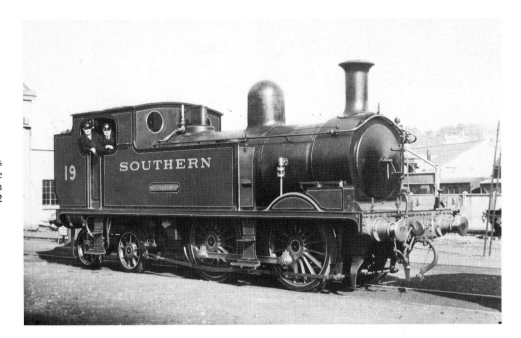

Plates 238 & 239 Two further views of 02 class 0-4-4T locomotives, fitted with larger style standard Island bunkers, in immediate Southern Railway livery. No. 19 *Osborne*, and No. 32 *Bonchurch* are seen at Ryde St. John's Road.

Plate 240 In 1946, the Southern Railway authorities gave considerable thought to the use of more powerful locomotives on the Island and, in particular, the possibility of using push-pull trains on the Ryde to Ventnor line. In December 1946, LBSCR Billinton large radial 0-6-2T No. 2510 was taken into Eastleigh Works for modification to Island loading gauge, which included the fitting of a shortened chimney. On 22nd February 1947, No. 2510 was shipped across The Solent from Southampton Docks to Medina Wharf and entered trial service, a few days later, from Newport. Unfortunately, because of tight clearances, No. 2510 was barred from the Ventnor line, although it took part in trials on all lines. The long-coupled wheelbase, tight clearances and poor braking, and the heavier coal consumption over the more flexible 02 class locomotives, meant that No. 2510 was soon relegated to the position of spare engine at Newport Shed, with use restricted to the Sandown to Cowes line. During its stay on the Island, No. 2510 succeeded in demolishing level crossing gates on the Freshwater line, due to poor brakes, and damaging the platforms at Newport and two other stations, due to tight clearance of the buffer beam and footsteps. No. 2510, ex-LBSCR No. 510, built in December 1900, was seldom steamed and returned in disgrace to the mainland on 14th April 1949 being finally scrapped in 1962.

Plate 241   To obviate the necessity of providing a locomotive specially to shunt Ryde Works, A. B. MacLeod devised a small manual tractor to move wagons about the yard. Built on a wooden chassis and platform *Midget*, as it was named, was carried on 4 small coupled wheels 14ins. in diameter, with a 5ft. wheelbase. On the wooden platform, two hand wheels were mounted on a centre column with a 2 speed gearbox of 1 to 1 and 1 to 4 ratio, with a chain drive. In low gear, *Midget* could move a load of 20 tons. Worked by two men, it proved useful in service, but was withdrawn in 1938.

Plate243 (left)   The Isle of Wight is renowned for its all the year round sunshine and, therefore, it is surprising to find an 02 class 0-4-4T locomotive experimentally fitted with a snowplough in 1933. The number of the locomotive pictured outside Ryde Shed is unknown, but it is certain that the snowplough was never used on the Isle of Wight.

Plate 242   Another experiment initiated by A. B. MacLeod was this fitment to E1 class locomotive No. 2 *Yarmouth*. In 1932/3, all Island locomotives were fitted with hinged cab doors, but the draught from the prevailing south-west wind, when shunting at Medina Wharf, rendered the E1 tanks unpopular with crews. The side screen was devised and fitted to No. 2 on one side only and folded back into the cab when not required. The experiment only lasted a few months and proved unpopular with crews, as the fitment took up too much room in the already cramped cab.

COACHING STOCK

Plate 244 The FYNR introduced a small 4 wheel petrol railcar into service in July 1913. Built by the Drewry Car Company, the body was of a semi-open type, capable of seating 12 to 15 passengers, on three cross bench seats which were fitted with reversible backs. The railcar could be driven from either end and was powered by a 20hp engine. The body of this unusual machine was built with a teak frame whilst the chassis was made from steel channelling which was braced by steel tube cross members. The engine and gearbox was carried on a detachable steel angle inner frame. The railcar was landed at Newport Quay and taken by a cart, drawn by a traction engine, to be put on the rails at Carisbrooke Station. It was utilized for passenger working on the line for just over a decade, though the Southern Railway, on takeover, found little use for the vehicle. Although, initially numbered as a normal third class carriage, No. 2462, it was then quickly transferred to service stock as inspection car No. 437S. It was broken up at Newport in 1927. The vehicle was often held in reserve when the Lymington steamer was delayed and was used for private hire at any time that the line was clear of traffic on payment of a minimum of four first class or eight third class fares.

Plate 245 One of the ex-Metropolitan Railway 8 wheel coaches purchased by the IWR in 1914 and numbered 22. The vehicle, with four third class and three first class compartments, was renumbered by the Southern Railway 6344 and included in train set No. 486. The vehicle is seen at Brading in 1929, the year of its withdrawal.

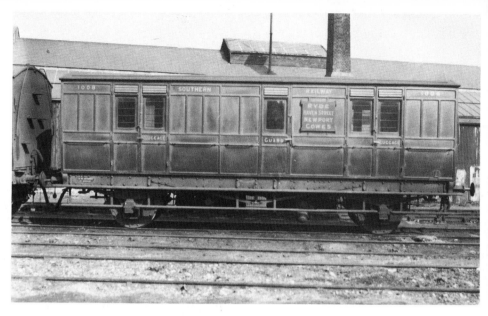

Plate 246 A 4 wheel full brake No. 1008, ex-SECR No. 440, and originally built by the London, Chatham & Dover Railway in June 1897. The vehicle was transferred to the Isle of Wight in May 1930, and served for twenty years on passenger services before being transferred to service stock in September 1950, as No. DS3105. It was broken up in October 1964. Pictured at Newport, No. 1008 displays the Island type exterior route indicator, for the Ryde to Cowes line, on the side panel.

Plate 247 Southern Railway saloon brake No. 4103. The vehicle was originally the carriage portion of IWCR steam railcar No. 1. Laid aside in May 1913, the carriage portion was given a second bogie, numbered 52, and used for normal passenger services. The vehicle was withdrawn in 1949 and received, during its lifetime, SR diagram No. 217.

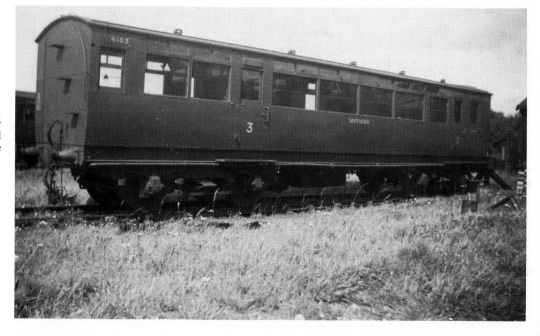

Plate 248 Saloon/brake No. 4103 seen in the later SR livery at Sandown, showing the steel panelling which replaced the ornate timber beading.

Plate 249 Ex-Plymouth, Devonport & South Western Junction Railway 46ft. bogie centre van brake third, No. 19, was transferred to the Island in June 1923 and is pictured at Ryde in May 1937 as No. S4107 (SR diagram No. 212). The vehicle was withdrawn in April 1939.

Plate 250 Ex-LCDR 6 wheel, converted to 4 wheel, five compartment full third, Southern Railway No. 2483, is seen at Newport in May 1937. The vehicle, fitted with short buffers and close-coupling drawgear, is typical of many vehicles which were transferred to the Isle of Wight by the Southern Railway after the Grouping. No. 2483 was built in 1891, was transferred to the Island in 1930, and was withdrawn in 1937.

Plate 251 Ex-LCDR 6 wheel, converted to 4 wheel, five compartment full third, No. 2487, fitted with normal length buffers and drawgear. Built in 1887, No. 2487 was transferred to the Isle of Wight in 1927 and was condemned in 1937.

Plate 252 Built originally as a 6 wheel vehicle by the LCDR in 1893, No. 4150 was transferred to the Isle of Wight by the Southern Railway in 1929, and served as a brake third. Before transfer, the centre wheels were removed and the vehicle was strenghtened by the provision of additional truss rods. No. 4150, shown at Newport in October 1935, was finally withdrawn in 1949. An ex-LCDR hearse van, No. 1010, is seen on the right.

Plate 253 Ex-London, Chatham & Dover Railway eight compartment third, No. 2428, was originally built in 1897 by the Gloucester Railway Carriage & Wagon Company. The vehicle was transferred to the Isle of Wight in May 1931 and served for eighteen years on passenger services before being withdrawn in April 1949. No. 2428 was then converted to a mess and tool van, No. DS3153, and was finally scrapped in 1955.

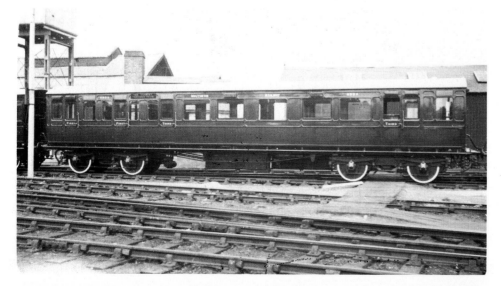

Plate 254 Built originally as an invalid saloon by the London Brighton, & South Coast Railway in 1916, first/third composite saloon No. 6986 was transferred to the Island in June 1934. It was included in a 4 set, together with the ex-IWCR railmotor coach, into a train which ran on the 'Tourist Express', throughout the summer months, from Ventnor or Shanklin to Freshwater and return. No. 6986, shown here carrying the 'Tourist' destination board, was withdrawn in 1959 and was subsequently rebuilt as breakdown van No. DS70008 (see page 83 of *Steam on the Isle of Wight 1956-66)*, before being scrapped in 1967.

Plate 255 On 15th June 1923, IWR 2-4-0T *Ventnor* leaves St. Helen's with a Bembridge train. The leading coach is an IWR 1864 four wheel birdcage brake third, either No. 1, 3 or 4, which was rebuilt at Ryde Works as a luggage van in 1906. The outside rodding to the brake, at the end of the vehicle, is worthy of note.

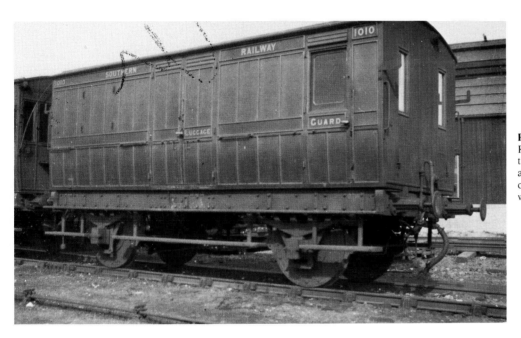

Plate 256 A London, Chatham & Dover Railway 4 wheel hearse van, built in 1884 and transferred to the Isle of Wight in 1931 as guards and luggage van No. 1010. This short vehicle, only 20ft. in length over headstocks, was withdrawn from traffic in 1937.

WAGONS

Plate 257 Works boiler truck, SR No. 439S, stands at St. Helen's Quay with an 02 class boiler, awaiting transit to Ryde Works. This vehicle was originally constructed at Ryde in 1920 by the IWR as car and container truck No. 76.

Plate 258 The Isle of Wight Central Railway introduced two water carrier wagons, and these remained in service with the Southern Railway and were rebuilt on LSWR frames as weed killing tanks. Nos. 428S and 443S are shown at Newport, in company with brake van No. ED472S, which was retained for use specially with the weed killing train.

Plate 259 Three ex-IWR 12 ton open wagons which were transferred to the Locomotive Running Department and CME in 1929. They are, from left to right: departmental locomotive No. 64393 (old SR No. 27456/old IWR No. 127) which was rebuilt at Ryde in 1913; departmental locomotive No. 64394 (old SR No. 27958/old IWR No. 154) which was built by Wheeler Bros., in 1915 and, departmental locomotive No. 64400 (old SR No. 27969/old IWR No. 225) which was also rebuilt at Ryde in 1913.

Plate 260 Ex-LBSCR 4 wheel horsebox, SR No. 3370, stands in Freshwater yard on 15th April 1950. Built by the LBSCR, to the design of Billinton, the vehicle was originally condemned in October 1924, but was reinstated by the Southern Railway as No. 3113 and transferred to the Isle of Wight in April 1925. Renumbered in the Island series, as 3370 in 1929, the horsebox saw little use after World War II and was withdrawn in 1955.

Plate 261 An SR 4 wheel tool van utilized by the Engineering Department's bridge section. Believed to have been of IWCR origin, the vehicle was sold to the Freshwater, Yarmouth & Newport Railway and became covered goods van No. 15. The vehicle, weighing 4 tons 11cwt., and capable of conveying a load of 8 tons, was renumbered by the Southern Railway, 47033, before being transferred to service stock in August 1930. Shown standing at Whitwell, the van was withdrawn in 1939.

Plate 262 This GER 10 ton cattle wagon was purchased by the IWCR about 1910 and renumbered in their fleet as 43. In 1927, the Southern Railway repaired and repainted the Westinghouse brake-fitted wagon and renumbered it 53385. Cattle traffic was, however, on the decline and this elderly vehicle only remained in traffic for a further seven years before its withdrawal in 1934.

Plate 263 Two variations of the LBSCR van used extensively, by the Southern Railway, on the Island's railway system. No. 46945 was built in 1915 originally as an 8 ton van but, on transfer to the Island in 1930, it was upgraded to a 10 ton general purposes van, before being lettered for fish traffic only. This van was condemned in 1946 and was then converted for departmental use as plumber's tool van No. 393S. It was withdrawn in 1955. No. 46960, built as a 10 ton van in 1922, was transferred to the Isle of Wight in 1929 and remained as a general purpose goods van up to its withdrawal in 1946. This van also saw further use as departmental van No. 388S before being scrapped in 1955.

Plate 264 LBSCR 10 ton van No. 46939, languishes in Godshill sidings, in 1950. This vehicle was originally built for 8 ton capacity in 1900 and was transferred to the Isle of Wight as a 10 ton van. The strengthening bar across the end of the vehicle is of particular interest.

Plate 265 The Southern Railway transferred ten 20 ton LBSCR dropside ballast wagons to the Island to assist the Civil Engineer in track maintenance. No. 62810, shown standing in No. 1 siding at Merstone, was built in 1904 but, according to records, was never officially transferred to the Island. It was withdrawn in 1955.

Plate 266 Three LBSCR 10 ton cattle wagons in unrebuilt condition, stand in the siding at Yarmouth. From left to right, Nos. 53372, 53371 and 53373 were all built in 1922 and were transferred to the Island in 1928/9. After World War II, they spent more time standing idle in sidings than in traffic, and were all condemned in 1956 spending their final years in the dump sidings at St. Helen's.

Plate 267 An LSWR road van, No. 56048, stands at Bembridge. Originally built in 1896, the van was transferred from the mainland in 1928 and was subsequently rebuilt with a second balcony and sanding gear, for use at Medina Wharf. No. 56048 was condemned in 1966 and was broken up in the ex-FYNR yard at Newport in July 1967.

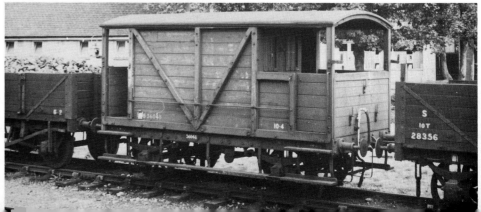

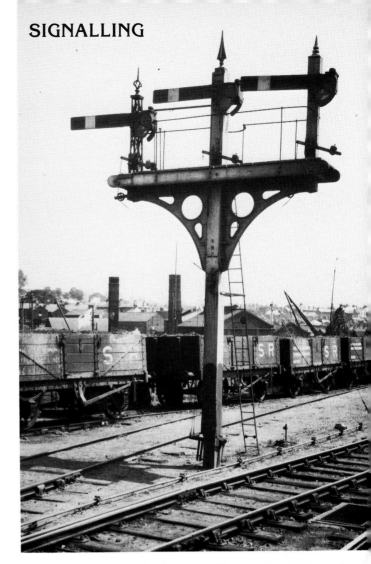

Plate 268 At the end of Ryde Pierhead platforms Nos. 2 and 3, was a gantry with starting and shunt ahead signals for all three roads and Ryde Esplanade's distant signal, whilst beyond this structure was a post with a bell on top, which was possibly used for starting trains. This remained in situ until 1967.

Plate 269 An ex-IWCR signal gantry at Newport, showing signs of Southern Railway modification, with ex-LSWR signal arms. The left-hand signal has a short LSWR lattice post. The three different styles of finial are clearly seen. The wagons in the background are all ex-IWR and were converted by the Southern Railway to motive power and M & EE use.

Plate 270 Watchingwell 'down' distant signal in 1951, with concrete post and LSWR/SR standard lower quadrant metal arm. This is one of the signals referred to in Plate 173 where passengers returned the signal to danger if they required a train to stop at Watchingwell.

Plate 271 The impressive array of signal gantries, situated north of Newport Station and controlled by Newport North signal box in 1920. The signals were supplied to the IWCR by the Railway Signal Company of Fazakerley, Liverpool.

Plate 272 At the Grouping, the Southern Railway found the Island railway signalling to be antiquated and, after the year 1923, replaced wooden posts and wooden arms with lattice posts of LSWR vintage and metal lower quadrant arms. Shortly after nationalization, a purge on signalling brought the introduction of upper quadrant arms and rail-built posts. At Sandown, however, the back platform 'down' starter to Shanklin was, in April 1950, still an IWCR vintage wooden post and wooden arm, complete with finial. E1 class 0-6-0T No. 4 *Wroxall*, in early BR green livery, shunts a 10 ton van and a large two verandah brake van, in the adjacent siding. The signal was replaced in 1952.

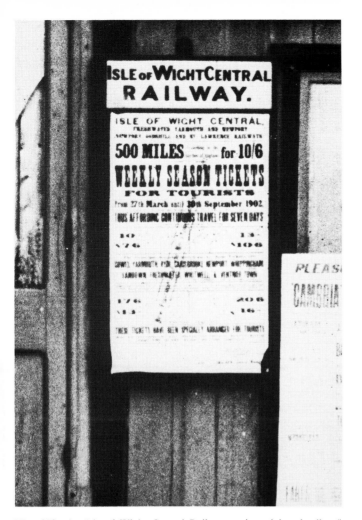

Plate 273 An Isle of Wight Central Railway notice, giving details of weekly Island travel tickets for tourists, priced at 10/6d in 1902. The facilities also included travel over the Newport, Godshill & St. Lawrence Railway and the Freshwater, Yarmouth & Newport Railway, (both worked by the IWCR) between 27th March and 30th September.

NOTICES

Plate 274 A Freshwater, Yarmouth & Newport Railway cast-iron boundary marker, at Newport, in 1935.

STAFF

Plate 275 The Joint lines committee employed a staff of twelve at Ryde Esplanade in the summer months which was reduced to eleven during winter time. In 1923, the annual wage bill totalled £1,738. This portrait was probably taken in the summer and included a lady employee (possibly a booking clerk).

TIMETABLES

Isle of Wight Central Railway.

WORKING TIME TABLE

FOR

October, 1909, and until further notice.

PRIVATE

For the information of the Company's Servants only.

General Offices, Newport, I.W.

CHAS. L. CONACHER, General Manager

RYDE LINE.

UP.

Miles	WEEK-DAYS.		1	2	3	4	5	6	7	8	9	10	11	12	13	14	SUNDAYS. 1	2	3	4	5	6
			Mail En (Mondays only. pass.)	Mail En (Mondays excepted.)	Mixed	Pass	Mixed	Lt.En	Mxd	Pass	Pass	Pass	LtEn.	Mixed	Mail	Pass (Satdys only)	Mail,En	Pass	Goods	Pass	Mixed	Pass
			a.m.	a.m	a.m.	a.m.	a.m.	noon	p.m	p.m	p.m	p.m.	p.m.	p.m.	p.m.	p.m	a.m.	a.m.	noon	p.m.	p.m.	p.m.
	NEWPORT	dep	2 30		7 25	9 25	10 25	–	1 10	3 10	5 0	5 45		8 0	8 45	9 15		10 15	12 0	2 40	4 25	8 20
2¼	Whippingham	A			7 30	9 31	10 31	–	1 15	3 15	5 5	5 ps 49		8 6	8ps49	9 20		10 20	12 7	2 45	4 30	8 25
3	Wootton	dep			7 33	9 34	10 34	–	1 18	3 18	5 8	5 52		8 10	8A51	9 24		10 23	12 10	2 48	4 33	8 27
4½	Haven Street	A			7 38	9 40	10 39	–	1 24	3 22	5 12	5 ps 55		8 16	8ps54	9 28		10 28	12 16	2 51	4 39	8 32
6	Ashey	A	2 45		7 43	9 43	10B44	–	1 28	3 26	5 16	5 ps 58		8E22	8ps57	9 33		10 32	12 22	2 54	4 44	8 37
8½	Ryde (St. John's Rd)	arr	—		7 48	9 48	10 50	...	1 33	3 32	5 22	6 C 3		8 29	9 3	9 40		10 39	12 30	2 59	4 50	8 43
8½	Ryde (St. John's Rd.)	dep	2 55	2 30	7 50	9 49	10 51	12 10	1 34	3 33	5 23	6 5	7 55	8 30	9 4		2 30	10 40	12 45	3 1	4 51	8 45
9	Ryde (Esplanade)	dep	2 58	2 33	7 54	9 52	10 53	12 13	1 37	3 37	5 27	6 8	7 58	8 32	9 7	—	2 33	10 43	12 48	3 3	4 53	8 47
9¾	RYDE (Pier Head	arr	3 0	2 35	7 56	9 55	10 55	12 15	1 40	3 40	5 30	6 10	8 0	8 35	9 10	—	2 35	1045	12 50	3 5	4 55	8 50

A Calls by Signal. B Cross No. 3 Down. C Cross No. 8 Down. E Cross No. 10 Down.

NOTES—Sundays—

No. 6 to conyey Mails, Vans to be left at Pier Head.

NOTES. Week-days.—No. 3 Must run to time to prevent delay to London Services.
Nos. 5, 7 & 12. Not more than one spring buffered wagon, with screw coupling, must be attached to these Trains without special authority. No intermediate Sidings to be worked unless ordered.
No. 14 Cross No. 11 Down at Ashey.

Ryde Goods Trains to run as per notice between 6 a.m. and 7 a.m.

ELECTRIC BLOCK. Newport, Wootton, Ashey. **TELEPHONE.** Newport, Whippingham, Wootton, Haven Street, Ashey, Ryde.

DOWN.

Miles	WEEK-DAYS.		1	2	3	4	5	6	7	8	9	10	11	12	13	SUNDAYS. 1	2	3	4	5	6
			Mail	Pass	Pass.	Lt.En	Mixed	Pass	Pass.	Pass.	Lt.En	Pass	Emp.	Mail En.	Pass. (Saturdays only)	Mail	Pass	Mixed	Pass.	Mixed	Pass.
			a.m.	a.m.	a.m.	a.m.	noon	p.m.	p.m	p.m.	p.m.	p.m	p.m.	p.m.	p.m.	a.m.	a.m.	p.m.	p.m.	p.m.	p.m.
	RYDE (Pier Head	dep	3 25	8 20	10 30	11 5	12 20	2 35	3 50	6 0	6 25	8 5	8 35	9 20		3 25	10 50	1 15	3 10	6 20	8 55
½	Ryde (Esplanade)	dep	3 30	8 22	10 32	11 7	12 22	2 37	3 52	6 2	6 27	8 7	8 37	9 22		3 30	10 52	1 17	3 12	6 22	8 57
1¼	Ryde (St. John's Rd)	arr	3 33	8 24	10 34	11 10	12 24	2 39	3 54	6 5	6 30	8 9	8 40	9 25		3 33	10 54	1 19	3 14	6 25	8 59
													Goods								
1¼	Ryde (St. John's Rd.)	dep	3D35	8 30	10 37	Shunt Ryde Yard.	12 30	2 44	3 59	6C10	Shunt Ryde Yard	8 14	9 30		9 45	3D35	10 57	1 22	3 18	6 28	9 5
3¼	Ashey	A	3E43	8 38	10B44		12 38	2 50	4 5	6 18		8G22	9 40		9 52	3E43	11 4	1 29	3 24	6 35	9 12
5	Haven Street	A	pass	8 42	10 48		12 42	2 54	4 9	6 22		8 26	9 45		9 56	pass	11 7	1 33	3 28	6 38	9 15
6½	Wootton	dep	pass	8 46	10 53		12 47	2 58	4 13	6 27		8 31	9 55		10A1	pass	11 12	1 38	3 32	6 44	9 20
7½	Whippingham	A	3F55	8 49	10 55		12 50	3 0	4 15	6 30		8 34	10 0		10 4	3F55	11 14	1 40	3 34	6 47	9 23
9¾	NEWPORT	arr	4 0	8 55	11 0		12 55	3 5	4 20	6 35		8 40	10 10		10 10	4 0	11 20	1 45	3 39	6 53	9 28

A. Calls by Signal. B. Cross No 5 Up unless late. C. Cross No. 10 Up at St. John's Road. G. Cross No. 12 Up.

NOTES.—Week-days.

No. 11 cross No. 14 Up at Ashey.
No. 1 D—Arrive on I.W.R. Road, cross over and pick up Tablet. E—Tablet and Staff. F—Stop for Bridge Test.

NOTES. Sundays

No. 3. Train Coaches of No. 12 Up, Saturdays, to be left at St. John's Road for this working, and cleaned there

STAFF SECTION. Newport to Ashey. **ELECTRIC TABLET.** Ashey to Ryde (St. John's Road).

VENTNOR LINE.

DOWN.

Miles	WEEK-DAYS.			1	2	3	4	5	6	7	8	9	SUNDAYS. 1	2
				Goods	Mixed	Pass.	Pass	Pass.	Exprs	Pass	Mixed	Pass (Saturdays)	Mixed	Pass
				a.m.	a.m.	a.m.	noon	p.m.	p.m.	p.m	p.m.	p.m.	a.m.	p.m.
	MERSTONE Jct.		dep	7 0	9 18	10 32	12 10	1 20	pass	5 35	8 15	9 24	9 30	8 34
1½	Godshill	A	dep	7 15	9 22	10 36	12 13	1 25	4 4	5 39	8 19	9 28	9 35	8 39
4	Whitwell		,,	7 45	9 29	10 41	12 18	1 31	4 A9	5 45	8 24	9 33	9 40	8 45
5½	St. Lawrence	A	,,	7 55	9 35	10 45	12 22	1 35	4 A12	5 50	8 31	9 37	9 45	8 50
6¾	VENTNOR Town		arr	8 5	9 40	10 50	12 25	1 40	4 15	5 55	8 35	9 40	9 50	8 55

A. Stops by Signal.

N.B. All Passenger Trains must stop momentarily outside Ventnor Home Signals—Goods Trains to stop dead.

NOTES. Week-days.

No. 1 Take all Ventnor Line Wagons Must work to time. Shunt Ventnor Yard on arrival. Load Sand when required. No. 3, 4, 6. & 8 Through Trains Cowes to Ventnor Town.

N.B.—See Main Line Sheet for Branch Engine Working.

ELECTRIC BLOCK. Merstone Junction, Godshill, Whitwell, Ventnor Town
TELEPHONE. Same, including St. Lawrence.

UP.

Miles	WEEK-DAYS.		1	2	3	4	5	6	7	8	9	SUNDAYS 1	2
			Mixed	Pass	Pass.	Pass	Mixed	Pass.	Pass	Pass	Pass (Sats. only)	Mixed	Pass
			a.m.	a.m.	a.m.	noon	p.m.	p.m.	p.m.	p.m.	p.m.	a.m.	p.m.
	VENTNOR Town	dep	8 25	9 45	10 55	12 30	2 35	4 45	6 0	8 40	9 45	10 35	9 0
1¼	St. Lawrence	A	8 30	9 50	10 59	12 34	2 39	4 49	6 4	8 44	9 49	10 39	9 4
2¾	Whitwell	dep.	8 35	9 55	11 3	12 38	2 43	4 53	6 8	8 48	9 53	10 44	9 8
5¼	Godshill	A	8 40	9 59	11 7	12 42	2 47	4 57	6 12	8 52	9 57	10 48	9 12
6¾	MERSTONE Jct.	arr.	8 45	10 2	11 10	12 46	2 50	4 59	6 15	8 55	10 0	10 52	9 16

NOTES.—Week-days. A Calls by Signal.

No. 1 to bring all Ventnor Line Wagons Heavy Engine. Must run to time.
No. 3 4. & 6 Must run to time. Through Trains to Cowes.
STAFF SECTION. Merstone Junction to Whitwell. Whitwell to Ventnor Town.

N.B.—Every effort must be made to work the Branch Trains to time, so that delay may not result to the Main Line Trains.

SANDOWN LINE.

DOWN. WEEK-DAYS.

Miles			1	2	3	4	5	6	7	8	9	10	11	12	13	14	15	16
			Goods a.m	Goods a.m	Mxd a.m	Mxd a.m	Pass. a.m.	Goods a.m.	Pass noon	Pas p.m	Goods	Pas p.m	Exp p.m.	Pass p.m	Pas p.m.	Mxd p.m	Goods p.m	Pass p.m.
	NEWPORT	dep.	6 30	6 45	7 40	9 5	10 20		12 0	1 5	(Newport to Shide 2-0 p.m.)	3 10	3 50	5 15	5 20	8 0	8 30	9 10
½	Pan Lane Siding	„	pass															
1	Shide	dep	pass	7 0	7A44	9A 8	10 A23		(Pass)	1 A9		3A14	pass	—	5A23	8 A 4	— (Saturdays excepted)	9 14 (Sats. only)
2¼	Blackwater	A		(Work Pan and Shide.)	7 47	9 12	10 26	B		1 12		3 17	pass	—	5 26	8 8	—	9 18
3¾	MERSTONE Junct.	arr	6 50		7 51	9 16	10 30		12 9	1 17		3 21	4ps0	5 25	5 30	8 12	8 45	9 22
3¾	MERSTONE Junct	dep	(To Ventnor)		7 53	9 18	10 32	11 15	12 10	1 20		3 23	(To Ventnor)	(To Ventnor)	5 32	8 15	9 15	9 24
5½	Horringford	A			7 57	9 22	10 36	11 20	12 14	1 24		3 27			5 36	8 19	—	9 28
6½	Newchurch	A			8 1	9 26	10 40		12 17	1 27		3 30			5 40	8 22	—	9 31
7¾	Alverstone	A			8 5	9 30	10 44		12 20	1 30		3 34			5 44	8 25	—	9 36
9	SANDOWN	arr.			8 10	9 35	10 48		12 25	1 35		3 38			5 48	8 30	9 45	9 40

DOWN. SUNDAYS.

Station	1	2	3	4	5	6
	Goods a.m.	Mixed a.m.	Pass p.m.	Mxd p.m.	Goods p.m.	Pass p.m
NEWPORT dep.	8 50	9 17	12 55	2 50	5 15	8 20
Pan Lane Siding						
Shide dep	9 5	9A21	12A59	2A 54		8A24
Blackwater	pass	9 24	1 3	2 58		8 27
MERSTONE Junct. arr	9 15	9 28	1 7	3 2	5 30	8 31
MERSTONE Junct dep	(Branch Engine)	9 30	1 9	3 4	5 45	8 33
Horringford		9 34	1 13	3 7		8 38
Newchurch		9 37	1 16	3 10		8 41
Alverstone		9 40	1 20	3 14		8 45
SANDOWN arr.		9 45	1 25	3 20	6 15	8 50

A Stops by Signal. N.B. Engines must not run coupled between Newport and Merstone Junction. N.B.—The maintenance of connection with I.W.R. Trains is of first importance

NOTES. Week-days. B.—Branch Engine work Horringford Pit if necessary.
No. 1 Take all Ventnor Line Wagons. Load sand as required. Shunt Ventnor Yard
No. 2 Engine of 7-25 Newport to Ryde. Work Pan and Shide to relieve Ventnor Goods.
No. 3. Convey Mew's and Crouchers Sandown Traffic.. No. 7 must run to time. Work through to Ventnor..

SUNDAYS.
No. 1 take empty Vectis Wagons to Shide Pit.
No. 5 leave on arrival of No. 4 Up. Worked by 3-45 p.m. Freshwater Engine.

ELECTRIC TABLET—Newport, Shide, and Merstone. ELECTRIC BLOCK—Merstone, Newchurch and Sandown.
TELEPHONE.—All Stations.

UP. WEEK-DAYS.

Miles			1	2	3	4	5	6	7	8	9	10	11	12	13	14	15	16	(unnumbered)
			Goods a.m.	Pass a.m.	Mixed a.m.	Pass a.m.	Goods a.m.	Pass p.m.	Goods	Mxd p.m	Eng. p.m.	Pass. p.m.	Pass p.m.	Pass p.m	Pass p.m.	Gds p.m	Pass p.m	Goods p.m.	Goods p.m.
	SANDOWN	dep.		8 30	9 45	10 55		12 30	(Shide to Newport 2-20 p.m.)	2 35	(From Sandown)	3 55	(Ex Ventnor)	6 0	8 40	(Sats. excepted.)	9 45 (Sats only.)	10 0 (Work as required) (Saturdays excepted)	(Saturdays only. Ex Ventnor Branch.)
1¼	Alverstone	A		8 34	(pass)	10 59		12 34		2 39		3 59		6 4	8 44		9 49		
2½	Newchurch	A		8 37		11 2		12 37		2 42		4 2		6 8	8 47		9 52		
3½	Horringford	A		8 41		11 5	11 35	12 40		2 45		4 6		6 12	8 51		9 55		
5¼	MERSTONE Junct.	arr		8 45	10 3	11 9	11 40	12 45		2 50		4 10		6 17	8 55		10 0		
5¼	MERSTONE Junct	dep		8 47	10 5	11 12		12 47		2 52	3 0	4 12	5 0	6 18	8 58	9 15	10 3	10 30	10 15
6¾	Blackwater	A		8 51	pass	11 16		12 52		2 57	—	4 17	5 4	6 22	9 2		10 8		A
8	Shide	dep	7 10	8A54	pass	11A20		12 A55		3 A1	—	4 21	5A7	6 A26	9 A 6		10A 12		A
9	NEWPORT	arr	7 15	8 58	10 15	11 24		1 0		3 5	3 10	4 25	5 10	6 30	9 10	9 30	10 15	10 45	10 30

UP. SUNDAYS.

Station	1	2	3	4	5	6	7
	Mixed a.m.	Goods a.m.	Pass. p.m.	Mixed p.m.	Goods p.m.	Pass p.m.	Goods p.m.
SANDOWN dep.	10 35	(Ventnor Branch)	2 15	4 40	6 30	9 0	(Ex Branch.)
Alverstone	10 39		2 18	4 44		9 4	
Newchurch	10 43		2 21	4 47		9 7	
Horringford	10 46		2 24	4 50		9 11	
MERSTONE Junct. arr	10 50		2 28	4 54	7 0	9 15	
MERSTONE Junct dep	10 54	11 5	2 29	4 57		9 17	9 30
Blackwater	10 59	11 10	2 32	5 2		9 21	
Shide dep	11A1	11 20	2A34	5A 5		9A24	
NEWPORT arr	11 5	11 25	2 37	5 8		9 28	9 45

A Stops by Signal. **N.B.—Engines must not run coupled between Newport and Merstone Junction.**

NOTES Week-days No. 3 Must run to time. Attach Wagons of No. 1 Up Branch at Merstone. No. 5 ex Horringford Pit if necessary. No. 6 must not be held at Sandown after 12-35 p.m. and work to Merstone only. No. 14 Return of 8-30 p.m. Goods from Newport.

TABLET SECTIONS. Newport, Shide, and Merstone. STAFF SECTION. Merstone Junction to Sandown.

Sundays.
No. 2 To clear out Shide and take up working of 12-0 noon Ryde Goods.
No. 5 Engine to work No. 2 Down Branch.

COWES LINE.

DOWN. WEEK-DAYS.

Miles			1	2	3	4	5	6	7	8	9	10	11	12
			Mail a.m.	Mixed a.m.	Pass. a.m.	Pass. a.m.	Pass. a.m.	Pass. p.m.	Pass. p.m.	Pass. p.m.	Pass. p.m.	Pass. p.m.	Pass p.m.	Pass. p.m.
	NEWPORT	dep	5 10	8 15	9 5	11 5	11 26	1 5	3 10	4 30	5 15	6 40	8 0	9 15
1½	Cement Mills	B	—	8 19	9 9	—	11 29	—	3 13	4 34	—	6 44	—	9 19
3	Medina Wharf	pass	5 19	8 23	9 13	11 11	11 33	1 13	3 17	4 39	5 22	6 47	8 8	9 23
4	Mill Hill	dep	—	8 28	9 18	—	11 38	1 18	3 22	4 43	5 26	6 53	8 12	9 27
4½	COWES	arr.	5 25	8 30	9 20	11 15	11 40	1 20	3 25	4 45	5 28	6 55	8 15	9 30

DOWN. SUNDAYS.

Station	1	2	3	4	5	6	7
	Mail a.m.	Pass. a.m.	Pass. a.m.	Pass. p.m.	Pass. p.m.	Pass. p.m.	Pass p.m.
NEWPORT dep	5 10	9 35	11 25	2 0	3 42	5 10	9 30
Cement Mills	—	9 39	11 27	2 3	3 45	5 14	9 34
Medina Wharf	5 19	9 43	11 32	2 6	3 49	5 18	9 38
Mill Hill	—	9 48	11 37	2 11	3 53	5 23	9 43
COWES arr.	5 25	9 50	11 40	2 13	3 55	5 25	9 45

Wharf Engine to work as required. N.B.—No Trains must cross at Medina Wharf in either direction. No. 1 to be worked by Wharf Engine. Must reach Cowes by 5-30 a.m. No. 5, 6, & 9 Week-days. must run to time. No. 6 not cal at Mills.
ELECTRIC TABLET. Newport, Medina Wharf, Cowes. TELEPHONE. Newport, Cement Mills, Wharf Box, Medina Wharf, Mill Hill, Cowes.

UP. WEEK-DAYS,

Miles			1	2	3	4	5	6	7	8	9	10	11	12	13
			Pass. a.m.	Pass a.m.	Pass. a.m.	Pass. p.m.	Pass. p.m.	Exprs p.m.	Pass. p.m.	Pass. p.m.	Goods p.m.	Mixed p.m.	Mail p.m	Pass. p.m. (Sats. excepted)	Pass p.m. (Sats. only.)
	COWES	dep	8 45	10 0	11 45	12 40	2 50	3 35	5 5	5 31	...	7 40	8 30	9 45	10 0
½	Mill Hill	dep	8 47	10 2	11 B47	12 42	2 52	3B37	5A 7	5 33	...	7 42	8B32	9 47	10 2
1½	Medina Wharf	pass	8 51	10 7	11 49	12 47	2 57	3 41	5 10	5 36	6 0	7 46	8 36	9 52	10 7
2¾	Cement Mills	B	8 54	10 11	—	12 51	3 0	—	—	5 40	6 15	7 49	—	9 56	10 11
4½	NEWPORT	arr	8 58	10 15	11 56	12 55	3 5	3 47	5 15	5 43	6 30	7 55	8 42	10 0	10 15

UP. SUNDAYS.

Station	1	2	3	4	5	6
	Pass a.m.	Pass p.m.	Pass p.m.	Pas p.m.	Pass p.m.	Pass p.m.
COWES dep	10 0	12 40	2 20	4 5	8 5	10 0
Mill Hill dep	10 2	12 42	2 22	4 7	8 7	10 2
Medina Wharf pass	10 6	12 46	2 26	4 12	8 10	10 7
Cement Mills B	10 9	12 49	2 30	4 16	8 13	10 11
NEWPORT arr	10 13	12 53	2 34	4 20	8 17	10 15

No. 4. must run to time. **N.B.—No Trains must cross at Medina Wharf in either direction.**
A. Saturdays only and other days at Station Master's discretion. No. 9. shunting Engine from Wharf, clear Mills. B. Calls by signal. No. 13 must connect with Southampton Boat.

N.B. Wharf Engine to work as required.

FRESHWATER LINE.

DOWN. WEEK-DAYS.

Miles			1	2	3	4	5	6	7	8
		Mail &	Goods a.m.	Pass. a.m.	Mixed a.m.	Pass p.m.	Pass p.m.	Mixed p.m.	Pass p.m.	Pass p.m. (Saturdays only.)
	NEWPORT	dep	4 30	9 2	11 30	1 10	3 15	4 35	6 40	9 15
1¼	Carisbrooke	dep	—	9 9	11A 37	1 17	3 A22	4 48	6 47	9A22
3¾	Watchingwell	A	—	9 14	11 42	1 22	...	4 53	6 52	9 28
5½	Calbourne	dep	4 50	9 19	11 A47	1A27	3A32	4 58	6A 56	9 32
6¾	Ningwood	dep	5 5	9 23	11A52	1A32	3A37	5 4	7A 1	9 37
9¾	Yarmouth	dep	5 30	9 32	12 0	1 40	3 45	5 10	7 10	9 45
12	FRESHWATER	arr	5 40	9 37	12 5	1 45	3 50	5 15	7 15	9 50

DOWN. SUNDAYS.

Station	1	2	3		
	Mail a.m.	Mixed a.m.	Pass. p.m		
NEWPORT dep	4 30	11 35	7 0	...	...
Carisbrooke dep	—	11A 42	7 7	...	...
Watchingwell A	—	11 49	7 14	...	...
Calbourne dep	4 50	11 A52	7 17	...	...
Ningwood dep	5 5	11A 55	7 21	...	...
Yarmouth dep	5 30	12 5	7 30	...	...
FRESHWATER arr	5 40	12 10	7 35	...	...

A Calls by signal.

NOTES.—Weekdays. No. 1 Take forward all Goods traffic. Unload Mails and shunt at Yarmouth as required. Must reach Freshwater by 5-45 a.m. Shunt at Freshwater and return with 8-15 a.m. train. No. 2 must work to time. No. 3. To convey none but urgent Wagons. No. 5 must work to time. Stop at Watchingwell for Tenants only. No. 6 Cross No. 5 Up at Carisbrooke. Train to be left at Freshwater for 8-15 a.m. working

SUNDAYS.
No. 1 convey Mails only. Return with No. 1 Up.

ELECTRIC BLOCK. Carisbrooke, Calbourne, Ningwood, Yarmouth and Freshwater. TELEPHONE. Same

UP. WEEK-DAYS.

Miles			1	2	3	4	5	6	7	8	9
			Mixed a.m.	Pass a.m.	Mixed noon	Pass p.m.	Mxd. p.m.	Goods p.m. (Sats. excepted)	Pass. p.m. (Saturdays only.)	Pass p.m.	Mixed p.m. (Saturdays only)
	FRESHWATER	dep	8 15	9 42	12 20	2 25	4 20	5 45	6 0	7 20	10 0
2¼	Yarmouth	dep	8 20	9 47	12 25	2 30	4 25	5 50	6 5	7 25	10 5
5	Ningwood	dep	8A30	9 55	12 33	2 38	4 33	6 5	6 13	7A 33	10A 14
6¼	Calbourne	dep	8A35	10 0	12 38	2 A43	4 38	6 13	6 17	7A 38	10A 18
8¼	Watchingwell	A	8 42	10 4	12 42	2 47	4 42	6 20	6 21	7 42	10A 22
10¾	Carisbrooke	dep	8 50	10 10	12 48	2A53	4 48	6 28	6A 27	7A48	10A 28
12	NEWPORT	arr	8 55	10 17	12 55	3 0	4 55	6 35	6 35	7 55	10 35

UP. SUNDAYS.

Station	1	2	3		
	Pass. a.m.	Pass. p.m.	Pass p.m.		
FRESHWATER dep	8 40	3 45	7 40	...	...
Yarmouth dep	8 45	3 50	7 45	...	...
Ningwood dep	8 53	3 58	7 53	...	...
Calbourne dep	8 58	4 2	7 58	...	...
Watchingwell A	9 2	4 6	8 1	...	...
Carisbrooke dep	9 8	4 12	8 8	...	...
NEWPORT arr	9 14	4 20	8 15	...	...

A Calls by signal.

NOTES. Weekdays
No. 2 must run to time.
No. 6 Goods Train except Saturdays. Cross No. 7 Down at Carisbrooke when work requires.

STAFF SECTIONS. Newport to Carisbrooke. Carisbrooke to Ningwood. Ningwood to Freshwater.

SUNDAYS.
No. 2 Engine to work Sandown Goods

General Note.—The times of Goods Trains are fixed to give the latest running allowed. Earlier running is not prohibited if line clear.

Acknowledgements

The publication of this volume would not have been possible without the help of many people who have been kind enough to assist. In particular, I should like to thank Roger Silsbury and Alan Blackburn for putting their vast photographic collection of Isle of Wight railway material at my disposal. Also I wish to express my thanks to the Isle of Wight Steam Railway Board and the Wight Locomotive Society Committee for granting permission to publish photographs from the A. B. MacLeod Collection and other items. Part of the profits from the sale of this book, will further the aims of the Isle of Wight Steam Railway. Lastly, special thanks to to my mother, for typing the manuscript.

Historical details have been checked with documents that are available but apologies are offered for errors which may, inevitably, have occurred.

Photographic acknowledgements:

Alan Blackburn Collection: Plates 3, 4, 5, 6, 7, 9, 10, 12, 13, 14, 15, 17, 19, 20, 21, 23, 25, 29, 30, 32, 34, 35, 36, 37, 38, 40, 42, 45, 49, 52, 53, 58, 59, 61, 64, 65, 69, 73, 74, 77, 85, 88, 96, 101, 102, 108, 109, 110, 112, 114, 121, 124, 127, 129, 135, 136, 137, 142, 145, 148, 150, 152, 153, 154, 157, 162, 163, 167, 169, 173, 187, 190, 192, 197, 202, 204, 207, 211, 214, 215, 217, 219, 220, 222, 227, 228, 232, 233, 238, 248, 259, 260, 268, 270, 272, 273 and 275.

Wight Locomotive Society: Plate 16.

Roger Silsbury Collection: Plates 11, 24, 27, 33, 39, 46, 48, 62, 66, 92, 95, 116, 117, 119, 120, 132, 143, 149, 159, 178, 195, 208, 210, 224, 225, 231, 235, 244, 257, 261 and 263.

O. J. Morris: Plate 218.

Pamlin Prints: Plates 177, 203, 264, 265, 266 and 267.

H. F. Wheeler: Plate 245.

H. Patterson Rutherford: Plates 56, 67, 70, 81, 91, 99, 125, 126, 144, 164, 165, 182, 186 and 271.

S. W. Baker: Plates 68, 194 and 274.

Aerofilms: Plates 18 and 28.

H. C. Casserley: Plates 22, 43, 47, 51, 75, 78, 79, 84, 93, 94, 105, 111, 113, 118, 122, 141, 151, 168, 189, 193, 201, 213, 249, 250, 252 and 255.

Real Photographs: Plates 26, 60, 76, 196, 205, 209, 221, 229, 230 and 262.

H. Gordon Tidey/Lens of Sutton: Plates 31, 44, 104, 123 and 212.

Photomatic: Plates 41 and 103.

LCGB/Ken Nunn Collection: Plates 50, 166 and 200.

Locomotive Publishing Company: Plate 97.

W. A. Camwell: Plate 161.

J. G. Dewing: Plates 54 and 269.

A. MacLeod/Wight Locomotive Society: Plates 55, 71, 72, 83, 98, 100, 106, 107, 115, 128, 146, 147, 158, 171, 191, 198, 216, 226, 236, 237, 239, 240, 241, 242, 243, 246, 247, 251, 253, 254, 256 and 258.

LGRP: Plate 156.

OPC Collection: Plates 57, 86, 87, 89, 90, 130, 131, 133, 134, 138, 139, 140, 160, 170, 175, 179, 180, 181, 183, 184, 199 and 234.

Author's Collection: Plates 1, 2, 80, 155, 176 and 223.

J. E. Kite: Plates 63 and 206.

J. H. Aston: Plates 82, 172, 185 and 188.